CONVERSATIONS MADE EASY

CONVERSATIONS MADE EASY

Building Your Playbook for Growing Sales and
CONNECTING WITH CUSTOMERS

CHRIS JENNINGS

HOUNDSTOOTH
PRESS

CONVERSATIONS MADE EASY
Building Your Playbook for Growing Sales and Connecting with Customers

FIRST EDITION

ISBN   978-1-5445-3827-3   *Hardcover*
         978-1-5445-3825-9   *Paperback*
         978-1-5445-3826-6   *Ebook*
         978-1-5445-4052-8   *Audiobook*

CONTENTS

———

MY STORY

———

In the LAX United lounge today, I took a moment to reflect on the hundreds of times I have been in the small offices that are there—on my way to talks for a company sales meeting or a group of business leaders somewhere in the US or Canada. About one thousand such events, at least, along with over two thousand companies that I have coached, and probably no less than fifty thousand individuals, give me a lot to reflect upon compared to my very first sales territory experience in 1985.

As I drove around my new territory in San Francisco, hired out of college by a very large company, I spent a lot of time in my head wondering if this was time well spent. *Am I in the right career? Does this have a chance of working? What are my alternatives to the job I am in?* I had identified about eight prospects to call on, and the first two or three promptly dismissed my offering. I don't remember them being jerks, but they might have been.

The fourth one said they were interested. They quickly got me invoices from their current vendor, and that same day I had a new customer. *Maybe this could work?*

As I think back over the history of my life, and even today, I still spend plenty of time in my head—thinking—as I believe most people do; however, what I would like to think helped move my results forward was much more about **doing** than **thinking**. From the age of about eleven, I had started knocking on doors to ask, "Do you want the snow in your driveway shoveled for ten dollars, or could I cut your lawn or do other yard work?"

If you find yourself reading this book, you are probably responsible for the modern-day version of what I did early on, or you might be a highly skilled professional who is asked to also grow and develop clients, or you lead a team of people that you would like to help become more accomplished. Whatever the case may be, I can promise you that over the next several pages, I will give you ways to make every conversation easier than it might be for you today.

This will allow you to pave the way for whatever future you are imagining and make the journey a lot easier than expected had you not stumbled onto this read.

That said, Kobe Bryant, Tom Brady, Sidney Crosby, Derek Jeter, Tom Hanks, Steve Jobs, Serena Williams, and Sheryl Crow all shared one thing in common. They were willing to do the hard work to become great in their field. They put time into developing their skills.

I hope to challenge and inspire you to give the same level of effort they did in their careers to accomplish great things in yours.

I promise to offer you everything I think you will need to be even more successful than you are today, and to do so in the fewest words and pages possible. For those of you who want to skip ahead or decide to reread a section, I am providing an outline of what is included in the six parts of this book, along with why we are headed there. Ultimately, we will all find that some things in life are simple if you take the right action. Let's get started.

PART 1: IT'S JUST A CONVERSATION

I will give you an outline of how to have healthy conversations with your customers and potential customers without gimmicks, cheesiness, high pressure, or anything else that you, or they, find objectionable.

You will get:

- Specific examples of what to say and what not to say
- Before-you-go warm-ups
- Ways to connect quickly with new people
- Structured agendas that lead to better outcomes
- The best questions to ask
- Strategies for getting to know the whole organization
- Insight about when and how to offer something new
- Ways to secure commitments and increase conversion rates
- Tips on turning new customers into lifelong friends and buyers

My goal for you is to just **BeUseful** in a way that allows your customers to appreciate the types of conversations they have with you without feeling pressured—while still winning business.

PART 2: DO SOMETHING

If you are stalling getting out there and taking action on what you should be doing, we will address procrastination and excuse-making and turn our attention to what we can control—our activities, our actions—and work through how we can go about getting more **Go Live** activities built into our day.

We will lay out specific ways to:

- Structure your week
- Get the best return on all your activities
- Build robust pipelines and greater confidence
- Hold yourself and others accountable

PART 3: WRITING YOUR OWN STORY

This part is devoted to developing more confidence in every situation that used to, or still does, cause fear, anxiety, or apathy. I will give you specific tools to grow into the person you have always wanted to be.

This section takes a walk through the emotional journey from *I just got started and am feeling super afraid about all of this,* to *I can't believe how easy this is now, and I wonder what I was ever bothered by.*

Your mental conditioning matters, your thoughts matter; it's better to program your own thinking rather than have it done for you.

PART 4: TEN SYSTEMS TO BUILD A GREAT PLAYBOOK

This section looks at the ten best systems to leverage the learning around you, become a real student of the game, and surround yourself with high performers that have a sincere interest and ability to help you and your team.

All sales leaders and every individual can develop the skills necessary to outperform their competitors through this ten-step delivery of the most influential systems and processes to help your organization.

PART 5: THE SALES LEADER TOOL KIT

This is the tool kit you need if your team is looking to you for what they should be doing, and you are wondering *How can I structure the organization for growth? What is my role in this? How can I keep up with it all?*

Critical team-building components include:

- How to train and develop a team
- CRM dos and don'ts
- Top 10/20 boards and managing a pipeline
- Running effective one-to-ones
- Compensation planning
- Sales team structure
- Staffing and working with the customer care team
- Ten laws for personal growth

PART 6: THE SALESPERSON'S TOOL KIT

This is every reference you have wanted to make sure you are fine-tuning your game to lead to better results.

You will learn:

- The best questions to ask
- Tools for listening

- Ways to quantify the prospect's challenges and opportunities using **HEARD**
- The power of "no" and what it can do for you
- How to earn respect by being the adult in the room
- When to offer choices
- Humility, curiosity, and skepticism—putting your audience at ease

CLOSING COMMENTS

Here you will find a wrap-up that demonstrates how to put this all to work and teach the lessons contained in here in order to better understand the concepts and start to help others around you. If you would like a cheat sheet to take notes on while you are reading, go to ChrisJenningsGroup.com and download the Trail Map-Sales Playbook from our resources page.

PART 1

IT'S JUST A CONVERSATION

———

All human beings have a natural style and manner of communicating. Everyone they talk to sees their individual style, along with their unique mannerisms, nuances, accents, stutters, misspoken words, or pet phrases. The world around you sees this as your authentic self and believes what you say.

That is, until you want something from the person you are talking to—then you change how you speak, and you become more careful with your words, your jokes, and your level of friendliness; your audience starts to realize that you want something, and they become more guarded around you, more judgmental, and perhaps distant and vague.

This section demonstrates how to make talking to anybody easier and more effective by giving you some guidelines for highly effective conversations, sales calls, team meetings, client or employee reviews, or any other endeavor you may take on.

While my focus here will be on offering your goods and services to paying clients, this is by no means the end of its application.

BeUseful...Now

I told you earlier that I am hoping to cram as much useful information into the fewest pages possible so that you might use this book as a reference to make any conversation go better, with more mutually rewarding outcomes.

I also hope you will teach this process to others on your team, in your home, and in your communities to further facilitate transparency and create dialogues with people, even if you do want something from them. There is nothing inherently wrong with wanting something from somebody; problems only start when you get overly attached to outcomes and become less authentic and genuine in your communications.

You might want to know where this comes from. If so, read on; if not, skip ahead a few paragraphs.

BACK STORY

I was watching a talk that Jim Collins (*Good to Great* and other great reads) gave to a group of business leaders, and he shared a story about how early on in his career as a management consultant, he was seeking advice from Peter Drucker, who was the hot guru at the time. They spent a day together, and at the end of the day, during their goodbyes, Peter leaned in and told Jim to be useful. I understand Jim signs most of his letters with that encouragement.

To me, being useful to customers, employees, family members, and friends is our purpose here on this planet. If we can focus on being useful, we can always fit ourselves to a good purpose. If we focus exclusively on what we want, we will throw any relationship out of balance and be met with frustration and disappointment from many.

Additionally, I wanted a detailed checklist that makes it easier to have a great conversation with anybody about anything. I believe today, far too many people shy away from conversations because they aren't sure what to say, and unfortunately, we over-rely on email or other cryptic methods of communication that don't effectively connect the dots for our audience or us.

In the book *The Checklist Manifesto*, Atul Gawande details studies of efficiency in hospital ORs and other places where it was a matter of life and death. The research concluded that any process guided by a checklist would run more efficiently than a process without a checklist, so that was built into our **BeUseful...Now** process.

Lastly, I like acronyms as a memory jog—BFD, KISS, LMFAO, to name a few. If you are willing to put this to use, I can virtually guarantee you will have the formula down inside of a few weeks.

Here we go.

B... Before You Go

Be Useful... Now

Before You Go

Expectations

Unique Connections

Set an Agenda

Explore Their World

Finding Time/$/Resources

Understand Who Cares

Let Them Know You

Next Steps

Onboarding

What Else Can We Do/Referrals?

I want you to have a thoughtful pre-call plan—written interesting questions to ask your audience that anticipate the objections or concerns they might have and ways to appropriately address those concerns.

Ideally, you would do a dry run with an objective third party (someone who is not attached to the outcome) who will provide feedback on how they might respond.

Practice what you are going to say and how you are going to say it.

Think it through: Do you need a PowerPoint, or are you better without one? If you need a PowerPoint, have you run through it enough times to know how best to use it? Do you need samples or not? A contract or not?

Make this a routine that you walk through before every important conversation, especially with new people, to minimize your social anxiety and theirs.

It's helpful to research their company on LinkedIn and be able to reference specifics from their website.

Demonstrate to them that you care about the conversation and the work you do by being very intentional with your preparation for the conversation.

E... Expectations

Be Useful... Now

Before You Go

Expectations

Unique Connections

Set an Agenda

Explore Their World

Finding Time/$/Resources

Understand Who Cares

Let Them Know You

Next Steps

Onboarding

What Else Can We Do/Referrals?

Having a healthy set of expectations is a great way to get what you want out of any meeting and avoid feeling crushed when you don't get what you want.

Expect to have a great conversation with your customer or prospect. Feel like you belong in the room or the Zoom—like you are the best person in the world to help them address their issues.

Expect them to respect your opinion and value everything you have learned about the impact you can have on their situation, regardless of whether or not they hire you.

That is where the expectations should stop. Don't put pressure on yourself to turn nothing into something. If this conversation turns into a deal, fantastic. If not, it's somebody new to add to your LinkedIn profile, it's another practice call, it's potentially a new referral source, and you have now expanded your network of people in the industry, which is an important part of your journey.

Keeping your expectations low is the key to your happiness and to a buyer not feeling pressured by an overly eager salesperson, which will scare them away from ever wanting to buy from you.

Magically, if you give them enough space to opt in, and they don't feel any pressure, your results and conversion rates will increase while you efficiently conserve mental energy and devote your energies to great customers and contacts who want your help.

U... Unique Connections

Be Useful... Now

Before You Go

Expectations

Unique Connections

Set an Agenda

Explore Their World

Finding Time/$/Resources

Understand Who Cares

Let Them Know You

Next Steps

Onboarding

What Else Can We Do/Referrals?

I hate corporate speak—using large words and general terms that sound professional and don't really mean anything.

> **Don't say this:**
>
> "We pride ourselves on delivering highly functional resources to better adapt in a competitive marketplace..." blah, blah, blah.

I love authentic conversations where direct language delivered in a real way creates a bond between two or more people based on the relatability of the words spoken and the way they were delivered.

> **Say this instead:**
>
> "Most companies I see pretty much suck at keeping the whole team in the loop. Every now and then, I see a team that really works well together, either because they got lucky, they have been together forever, or they really do care more about the team than themselves. Any of that at all familiar?"

Finding ways to connect with an audience of one or many is key to keeping somebody listening and engaged. Let's face it, staying focused on any conversation can be challenging, let alone if you are in a sales role.

Speak the truth, and it will change the dynamic.

- If you interrupt somebody, call yourself out before they do.
- If they don't know or trust you yet, put a spotlight on that before they do.
- If they have been burned in the past by unreliable, overpromising salespeople, then tell them the odds are stacked against this going anywhere.

Being painfully honest, authentic, and relatable are the keys to standing out. This takes a risk, yes, but the payoff is tremendous.

I stumbled into this early in my career. I was about to graduate from UCLA with a bachelor's degree and was planning to move back to the New York area and find a job, most likely in financial services. In the meantime, I decided to apply to some of the larger companies coming onto campus to at least get some experience interviewing. I wasn't really looking for a job yet—I just wanted to tune up my interviewing skills since I was so new to the business world.

I interviewed with three large companies and got two job offers. Crazy! One of the hiring managers was Jack Muellerleile, the local District Manager for SoCal—the fifth largest company in the world at the time.

Jack said, "Tell me about yourself and why you think we should hire you."

I replied, "Well, when I got to campus as a seventeen-year-old freshman, I got really distracted from school. I had a lot of fun, dated a lot, drank far too many beers, and generally had the greatest time of my life. My grades were terrible, and I was making very little progress toward graduating. Starting with fall quarter last year, I got serious. I crammed three years of college into fifteen months and got the best grades of my life. I am ready to go to work. I think I have great potential, and I need a place where I can learn the business and fine tune my skills, and I am ready to go."

He called me a couple days later and said he was arranging for me to ride with one of the local reps who was doing great and had big potential like he thought I did. He said, "I loved your honesty—'I partied my butt off, and I'm ready to get busy with life.' I loved that."

I later found out that if Jack Muellerleile sponsored you, you basically had to no-show on your interview to not get hired.

Jack and I had a **Unique Connection** not based on pretense, inflated vocabulary, ego, or anything other than brutal honesty delivered in a meaningful way.

Get over your fear of not sounding "professional," and

Say this instead:

"I'm sure I caught you buried with a ton on your plate, this will be brief."

"It's a long shot, but I felt like I owed you a call."

"You may be way too far down the road with your current provider, but on the off chance we should talk, I wanted to reach out."

"I'm guessing you were hoping this would come in a lot less, and before you start yelling at me, I thought we should talk."

Learning how to do this by design and connect with a boatload of people who would have otherwise written you off as one of the many nondescript, vanilla-sounding people who are easy to forget about, will take you far in your career.

S... Set an Agenda

Be Useful... Now

Before You Go

Expectations

Unique Connections

Set an Agenda

Explore Their World

Finding Time/$/Resources

Understand Who Cares

Let Them Know You

Next Steps

Onboarding

What Else Can We Do/Referrals?

Set an agenda. I know that sounds ridiculously basic; as I sit here writing this, I am thinking to myself, *Why do I have to point out that this matters?* But the reality is almost nobody does it. At least on sales calls. Too often, we are not taking charge. I think it's because we are being polite or would rather do whatever the customer wants.

Please remember that you are the expert. You do this all the time. Your prospect may only buy this occasionally, perhaps they have never bought this before, and even if they have, they probably have a misguided way of going about it.

Keep it simple, but lay out a pathway forward.

> **Try something like this:**
>
> "Phil, appreciate the invite. Was super interested in what you guys do, and in prepping for the call today, I spent the last few days researching your company. I interviewed a couple of competitors and came up with a bunch of questions based on what I learned. Hopefully I can run those by you."
>
> "Guessing you have questions for me, happy to tackle any of those."
>
> "Based on how our Q and A goes, if I can think of some decent recommendations, I'm happy to share them with you."
>
> "Would love to get your immediate feedback on any suggestions I come up with, even if you don't like my suggestions."
>
> "How does that sound to you?"
>
> "Did I leave anything out that you can think of that we should address?"

Sometimes I recommend sending agendas in advance—but keep them short. Build them into the Outlook invite you send. For example:

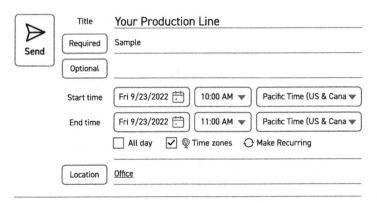

	Title	Your Production Line
Send	Required	Sample
	Optional	

Start time	Fri 9/23/2022 📅	10:00 AM ▼	Pacific Time (US & Cana ▼
End time	Fri 9/23/2022 📅	11:00 AM ▼	Pacific Time (US & Cana ▼

☐ All day   ☑ 🌐 Time zones   ↻ Make Recurring

Location	Office

Meeting details:

- Review downtime causes
- Identify equipment issues
- Delivery schedule

E... Explore Their World

Be Useful... Now

Before You Go

Expectations

Unique Connections

Set an Agenda

Explore Their World

Finding Time/$/Resources

Understand Who Cares

Let Them Know You

Next Steps

Onboarding

What Else Can We Do/Referrals?

Once again, everybody in sales knows to ask questions. I think, too often, the process gets overly formulaic and rote. If we stop thinking of the sales process as a sales process and think of it more like getting to know somebody and as many intimate details of their working world as we can, we have a better shot at gaining their trust and confidence.

Reality check here—do you really have a **genuine interest** in your customers' and prospects' businesses and lives? If you don't, do something else.

The key is to **develop a genuine curiosity** about the people you call on and the situations they encounter to help them assess whether or not they need to make any changes.

My wife, Lenna, is the sweetest person I have ever met. She has such a genuine, caring way about her, and when she talks to anybody, they can tell that she is truly interested in their story. My point is that we need to stay authentic and genuinely take an interest in others; your audience will know whether or not you really care.

You may find out quickly that, for various reasons, we shouldn't be talking, but the process of the conversation makes you more alert to what is important and helps you move away from what isn't important.

Many of us want to go fast—it does take more time to go deeper into the details of peoples' lives. Many of us don't have the patience to slow down. Keep in mind, we all have to manage the clock and fully explore the details of the most relevant areas of your prospects' lives, so you can have time to fit it all in.

Some prospects you call on will be like me: impatient. However, also like me, if it is important, they will give you all the time you need to help them diagnose and fix, or significantly improve, the quality of a problem or situation that you are prepared to address.

Think of every new customer like a puzzle. When you first open a new puzzle, you pour it out on the table. You start by turning over the pieces that show you cardboard versus the painted surface. Next, you look for the corners, then start getting the straight edges grouped together in some sort of line, followed by grouping together some of the obvious colors, and slowly, piece by piece, you build out the picture represented on the box.

The difference here is that there is no answer key. Don't assume they will want to give you everything at once. But if you are sincerely interested, they will open up and describe their story in intricate detail, allowing you to paint a picture of their life—as you see it— and suggest alterations in a meaningful way.

Make the questions unique to you, your customer, your industry, and their situation. Constantly look for feedback as to whether you are assessing things accurately. Think of what you really want to know about them and then ask.

While we do have a list of good questions later in the book, I am more interested in you creating tailor-made questions that help you get an idea of who your prospects are as people, how the product or service fits in their work and/or home life, and any other details they can give you.

Summarize everything they tell you constantly throughout the conversation.

When you think you know everything you need to know, ask:

"Is there anything else you think I should know?"

You may have to ask this several times; there is always more to know. Taking the time to do this deeper dive will put you in rare company, and you will start to edge out the overly eager, self-serving salespeople your customers are used to talking to.

Let's keep going.

F... Finding Time/ $/Resources

Be Useful... Now

Before You Go

Expectations

Unique Connections

Set an Agenda

Explore Their World

Finding Time/$/Resources

Understand Who Cares

Let Them Know You

Next Steps

Onboarding

What Else Can We Do/Referrals?

Details, details, and more details. Put together the whole puzzle, keep digging.

Let's assume your new prospective customer has given you some idea of what is missing in their work or life, and you are starting to see how what you do could improve their situation and make their lives easier. BTW, that is your job—to somehow make other people's lives easier or better. Based on your unique set of capabilities and offerings, if implemented, you should improve your customers' lives—if not, get out of their way, and let them find somebody else who can.

BACK TO FACT FINDING

There are **three basic facts** that need to be established:

1. **Time:** as in time to invest in fixing the problem
2. **Funding:** where their money comes from and how much they are ready to invest
3. **Resources:** meaning resources that you don't provide and they don't control

Let's tackle time first. When anybody makes a change, explores working with somebody new, or investigates a new offering, system, or task, there must be a time commitment.

In most cases, it's not a huge commitment, but it does need to be addressed. So, before you go into a capabilities presentation, create a scope of work, or put serious time into winning any new piece of business, get their commitment to put in the time with you—both during the sales process and after the purchase (if it goes that way).

It's a small commitment on their part, and it starts the psychology of them believing in and getting behind working with you while eliminating any post-demo nonsense of, "Well, we really like what you have to offer, only problem is the timing is really bad. We are just sooooo busy, I am sure you understand." As I said, nonsense.

No, we don't understand. Why would you have me run all over town, bother several people in my company to get you what you needed, and then shamelessly backpedal out of doing something with us? I know you are thinking this, but I don't suggest saying this.

However, you have to **look in the mirror** here. Ask yourself, *What did I do—or not do—that could have made this better?*

Keep asking that question. Stop blaming your prospects or customers; own your part of this equation, and you will get a lot better, a lot faster. Oh yeah, and when you think you have it all down. Think again.

One of my favorite coach's sayings is, "It's what you learn after you know it all that counts." So, for any of us egocentric types—yes, I said us—stay open to learning the lesson in every interaction and enjoy a full lifetime of never-ending growth and development.

People who live that way tend to make much more money than people who don't.

FACT FINDING PART 2

It's another **F** word—wait for it...**Funding**, oh yeah, **Funding**. Before we hear:

- "It's not in our budget at this time."
- "We get this done elsewhere for much less than what you charge."
- "We are sending this out to bid."
- "Your pricing is a little outside of what we are used to paying."

Or any of the other nonsense that goes on here, we need to get ahead of these common problems—before they become real issues and everybody's feelings get hurt, mostly yours. Salespeople are so sensitive, acting outwardly confident but inwardly second-guessing ourselves. More on that later.

> **Do Not Say:**
>
> "What's your budget?"

You are likely boxing yourself into an unrealistic fantasy target price they have in their head, which could be completely made up. I recently asked somebody who was looking to rent out space in a property we owned, "How much do you normally pay to rent a conference room in a hotel for a day?" He answered, "$200 to $300 per day." I basically laughed at him and said, "I don't know what kind of place you have been going to, but I have never rented a hotel conference space for less than $1K to $2K per day, if not a lot more, plus food and drink."

The concept of **Setting the Anchor** states that the first actual number brought up will likely be within 15 percent of where the final number lands.

So, if they set a budget of $5K, odds are the price ends up being somewhere between $4,250 and $5,750, and you work toward their number.

If you throw out an early $20K rough number, odds are the price ends up being closer to between $17K and $23K.

Oddly enough, it could be for the same type of product. Some people call this price conditioning. I call it being honest and being the adult in the room. If you sense, early on, that they can't afford you, you need this information to get out of there sooner rather than later.

If they can afford you but you wait too long and they throw out a ridiculously low number (which happens often), then they are forced to defend that ridiculously low number, even if they are full-on lying to you.

Be the adult, get real right from the start, and throw the number out before you ask them to commit to anything. Get the two of you on the same page about real dollars, and handle all sales conversations in real dollars, not percentages.

For example:

"Hey, before you sink $20K into doing this differently, how much in real dollars do you think it's costing you to do it the old way?" Get real dollars, not percentages. Them telling you, "It's probably costing us about five percentage points," is not the same as them saying, "It probably costs us at least $5 million per year in lost revenue."

FACT FINDING PART 3

This part is about other **events**, **resources**, or **prerequisites** that must happen in advance of you getting hired to do whatever you do.

We are trying to avoid the following:

- "We really want to hire you and implement this, but...
- "First, we need to install our new accounting system...
- "We are selling the company and will want to ask the new owners...
- "Would love to sign, but first, we need to get permits from the city...
- "We have to wait for offers to buy a new property to get that accepted and built out...

...and then we can get started."—ughhhh!

So simply get ahead of this in your fact finding with any of the following appropriate statements or questions:

- "Did you guys already get permits?"
- "Do you think your current accounting system can handle the changes?"
- "Any projected changes in ownership status that would deprioritize this?"
- "Do you even have enough space and capacity to incorporate this now?"

Just get ahead of everything. Bravely ensure that there are no real or make-believe obstacles that could slow this train down.

Doing so will also get your prospect behind the idea and help them see the clear path forward, thus increasing their commitment to the project, which can only help—or help you bail out early if there is something real in the way.

U... Understand Who Cares

Be Useful... Now

Before You Go

Expectations

Unique Connections

Set an Agenda

Explore Their World

Finding Time/$/Resources

Understand Who Cares

Let Them Know You

Next Steps

Onboarding

What Else Can We Do/Referrals?

Identifying stakeholders, decision-makers, and other interested parties is not a new concept.

The longer you are in your business, the better you will get at identifying common roadblocks and great ways to eliminate them or minimize their negative impact on your deal flow. This is another reason why I encourage you to stay in your field, get good at the nuances of it, and get really effective at finding deals more easily. If you hate the field you are in, then get out and move on to the next best opportunity that fulfills you.

Back to topic.

Understanding who else cares about the topic at hand is important; it's likely that many people who are impacted by what you offer care about changing suppliers, providers, etc.

> **Do not say this:**
>
> "Are you the ultimate decision-maker as it relates to this purchase?"

There is no good answer to this horrid question. People will be forced to lie and say, "I am" or feel undervalued, and say, "We make decisions as a team, and it is MY JOB to collect the information and pass it on to my internal stakeholders."

Either answer is bad for you and only sets you up for either folding and not saying anything—not a good option for full-grown adults—or going to battle with them over their assertion of how they do things there.

Say this instead:

"Anybody else here have an opinion on the topic?"

"Anybody going to feel left out if we didn't include them in the discussion?"

"Anybody going to get their feelings hurt if we didn't get their thoughts on the subject?"

"Anybody likely to cause trouble for you, if this turns out to be something that you want to do?"

"How much bureaucracy are you facing if it turned out that you wanted this kind of help?"

"Do you figure things out in a committee around here?" If yes, continue with, "Oh no, that must be hard for you, how much extra work do you end up doing as a result?"

Any of those above questions will set up a good dialogue. People talk a lot about internal champions; I would flip this around and say something like, "Hey, I don't want you to take on a fight that can't be won here. So, if you think this is a good idea, maybe you could fill me in on what historically has worked for you when getting new ideas approved and actually implemented versus getting talked about forever and you still not getting what you want?"

Keep it real. Keep it genuine. Keep it about them, not about you!!! If you know the names of all the stakeholders and can talk to them directly, then you are ready to keep moving forward. Without that, slow it down, and dig deeper for that information. Normally, the sooner you start looking at **Understanding Who Cares**, the better off you will be.

L... Let Them Know You

Be Useful... Now

Before You Go

Expectations

Unique Connections

Set an Agenda

Explore Their World

Finding Time/$/Resources

Understand Who Cares

Let Them Know You

Next Steps

Onboarding

What Else Can We Do/Referrals?

Sooner or later (later is usually better), if you have a reasonably well-qualified prospect where you see some real opportunity to improve their lives, their company, and the lives of their people, you are going to need to give them some idea of why you and why now.

A couple of ground rules on making presentations:

1. RESURFACE THE ISSUES

If you did all the other steps in a separate conversation, perhaps days or weeks prior to the time you get to tell them what you do, **resurface all the issues** you identified while *exploring their world* in a short summary.

"Last time I was here, you told me X, Y, and Z. Did I get that right?"

2. FOLLOW UP

Be ready to **ask a follow-up question** regarding the issues they shared last time. For example, "Last time we chatted, you mentioned that you were tired of using multiple systems to store data. Is that still the case? Or did you find a way to improve your situation since the last time we talked?" Let them answer, and then dig a little into areas that perhaps you hadn't fully explored.

"Out of curiosity, how much time do you think gets burned working in two systems?"

"Is it just you who has that experience, or are there others who feel the same way?"

Bottom line is, don't go in cold to a presentation without warming them up again as to the reasons why they are even talking to you. No matter how many reasons they gave you the last time you talked, there is a good chance they forgot what you talked about or had a bunch of other pressing issues since then that they are dealing with, and your opportunity may be devalued in the maze of business.

3. INCLUDE STAKEHOLDERS

If there are **new people, stakeholders**, etc., included in the presentation, make sure that after you spend five-ish minutes restating what was already covered, you ask anybody new if they agree with what you have learned, if there is anything they would like to add, or if they see any of it differently. Take your time here and give them openings to clarify their perspective so there is unanimous agreement on some of the core issues you would like to fix for them.

4. USE SOUND BITES

Think **thirty-second and sixty-second sound bites** that you deliver with absolute conviction of what you know to be true for you, your existing clients, and your potential new customer.

Make sure you have real passion and connection to anything you offer, even if it might seem trite or commonplace.

"The reason I got into the kitchen design business is I am a freak about having a well-organized kitchen, and I take a lot of pride in delivering the same for my clients. You told me you are so tired of having to search around the entire kitchen to find a pot, pan, or plate while, in the meantime, your dinner is burning on the stove. So, I designed this layout with that in mind, with a place for everything you would need within arm's length of the stove while still giving you the light from the window at your back to better see what you are doing. I think this will make a huge difference for you when entertaining or even on an everyday basis."

Or:

"My favorite part of technology is when I get to save somebody like you—and perhaps your whole team—a bunch of time over the course of the average day or week. You told me that having dual operating systems, which initially made sense, got old a long time ago and that you are burning way too much time bouncing back and forth.

"So we designed this system to seamlessly transfer all your existing data into one location; it syncs with your accounting platform and your ERP system, so my guess is not only will you save about two hours a week, but all one hundred people in your division will have the same savings, so roughly two hundred hours per week saved, which I think is like getting back a whole month's worth of productivity every month across your division. Now, there will be a ramp-up, but inside of three months, I think you and your team may be able to breathe again."

5. MANAGE THE CLOCK

Any time you offer an idea, ask for feedback, or make a presentation or demo, you must leave about fifteen to twenty minutes to have some back and forth, ask and answer clarifying questions, etc. For example, in a 1:00 p.m. meeting scheduled to end at 2:00 p.m., if you don't wrap up whatever you need to tell them by 1:45, you are in trouble, and you increase the odds of them saying, "Wow, you gave us a lot of great stuff to digest, I am running late for my next meeting, so give me some time to consider this and check back with me later in the month."

This is a major problem! If this is happening to you a lot, then I would guess your conversion rates are lower than they could be, your sales cycle is dragging on, and your pipeline is less secure than it could be.

Ideally, there is ample time to get to a conclusion in this one meeting, and they are saying, "This is great; let's get started. Can you sign our NDA? Let's set up a kickoff call."

If this isn't what happens to you most of the time, then you are allowing for more sales dysfunction than is necessary; let's try to tighten it up.

6. CLOSING THE SALE

Complete silence at the end isn't a terrible sign, but it may not be great. I am not a giant fan of the tired old "closing statement" such as, "If I could show you a way, would you buy today?" "What do you say we get started?" "Can I get your commitment to buy now?" Yuck, puke, disgusting.

Say this instead:

"I'm interested in your thoughts."

"Would appreciate your feedback."

"What are you thinking at this point?"

"Does any of what I have covered sound appealing, or did we completely miss the mark?"

"Not sure if any of this is resonating with you?"

"Did we come close to what you thought you might want or are we still way off?"

There really isn't any magic closing phrase that doesn't sound contrived; I would encourage you to find things to say from this list or others that fit your personality and setting.

7. PAY ATTENTION

If you don't come to a conclusion in this meeting, no matter what, PAY ATTENTION!!!

If they didn't say, "Let's get you a PO and start," and they didn't say, "This is a pathetic pile of junk, can't believe you have any customers at all," **get a date and time on the calendar to come back and finish the conversation.**

DO NOT accept, "Give me a couple weeks, and I will let you know," "We are still waiting for other quotes to come in; call me around the first," or, "This looks great; I have some internal work to do, give me about a month."

Whatever they say, **respond with something like the following:**

"Completely makes sense to me; sounds like you need some time to figure out how and if this fits?" They will likely say, "Yes, thanks, that sounds great."

You say, "No problem, sounds like you have a week or two worth of digging into this to do. Is that about right?" Wait for confirmation of their time frame. Then continue, "Sounds like we will need to regroup later in the month, maybe the week of the twenty-first? Are you even around that week?" Wait for them to open their calendar and say, "Yes, that week is good."

You say, "Any day that week better for you? Maybe Wednesday or Thursday the twenty-third or twenty-fourth?" Once they say that day is good, or offer you an alternate day, ask, "What time is good for you?"

They will offer a time.

> **Say something like this:**
>
> "OK, I will send you an invite for Wednesday the twenty-third at 10:00 a.m. I'm going to hold an hour for you in case you have any detailed questions. If it turns out that you have a different idea, it may end up being a much shorter conversation, which is fine. In case it turns out you are eager to get started, I will be prepared with some initial items to help you launch quicker. If you like, perhaps bring your IT manager along so we can map out a plan for the integration?"

Give them some ideas of what they could do to accelerate the "getting started" phase but reassure them it's not necessary; only offer it to help them move faster **if** they are so inclined.

If you do all the things listed above, your odds of getting deals instead of excuses and shortened timelines should improve, perhaps a lot.

There are some very important subtleties here (please see **Part 6 Salespersons Tool Kit**).

N... Next Steps

Be Useful... Now

Before You Go

Expectations

Unique Connections

Set an Agenda

Explore Their World

Finding Time/$/Resources

Understand Who Cares

Let Them Know You

Next Steps

Onboarding

What Else Can We Do/Referrals?

The **"Now" in BeUseful…Now** largely applies only to new customers and/or opportunities that are more complex, requiring several stages in your sales process. If the deal is already over, or you want out, get a referral and keep moving. If it is a complex deal, and/or you have already secured the business, let's continue.

This section will be simple if you are not zoning out too often while you read. I do that often and have to repeat the section. I have already given you the answer here. Remember what it is?

Absolutely every time you talk to a prospect, make sure you get a **DATE and TIME** on both of your calendars where you can figure out if you offer a viable answer to your prospect's issues.

At the end of call number one, they say, "This is great; I like this. Let me take a closer look at what you have, your web page, your online tutorial, my committee." Blah blah blah.

Your response is pretty straightforward:

Acknowledge what they said, "So it sounds like you want to check with the team and go over the tutorial together?" The prospect says, "Yes, I think that will help us." You say, "Sounds good; how long do you think that will take you?" You want to ask this **first**, so you don't try to nail down a time that doesn't fit their schedule.

They say, "Give me a week."

You say, "Sounds good, so we need to regroup probably the week of the twenty-first?"

They say, "No, give me two weeks," or they say, "Yes, that's right." In either case, you restate what needs to happen.

"So, it sounds like we are looking at the week of the twenty-eighth. How are you looking mid-day on the twenty-ninth? Or later, the thirtieth?"

At this point, they are in their calendar.

They say, "The twenty-ninth at 11:00 a.m. is great."

You say, "Got it. I'll shoot you an invite for the twenty-ninth at 11:00 a.m. Anybody else you want to invite to the party?"

Wait and see if we have new players. This could be important for you to get a heads up on why and where they fit in (see prior section **Understand Who Cares**).

They say, "No, just the three of us and your team."

You say, "OK perfect; I have us down for the twenty-ninth at 11:00 a.m. We can walk through whatever you learn between now and then and decide if we have anything to get started on or not. If you like, I will bring _____ from my implementation team, so they can be prepared for whatever we might do together. If any questions come up prior, you know how to reach me.

"Maybe you could send me _____." It's good to have them get you something else that moves the whole deal forward; it's another small commitment prior to the larger commitment, which gets them in the habit of making commitments to you and honoring them.

The only other thing you might do here is address a roadblock they are likely to encounter and offer them some reassurance that you still want to talk to them:

"If it turns out your accounting team is unwilling or unable to figure out how to pull up the info we need, either let me know prior or bring one of them to the call so I can help and make it easier to do."

This, done right, should eliminate 90 percent of the frustrating follow-up that goes nowhere—the string of annoying unanswered emails, voicemails, passive LinkedIn messages, and other nonsense that we do.

If they aren't willing to book that follow-up rendezvous, then you should really be asking yourself, and more importantly, your prospect, *Is this really something they want to be looking at right now, or did we just venture down a path that isn't really helpful for them?*

Give them an out. I always say, "**At the first sign of hesitation. Give them an out!**" It will get them really honest, really fast, and then you make a business decision. Do I want to pursue this or not?

> **Something like this:**
>
> "I get it. Do me a favor; if you think this really doesn't belong on your priority list or, for that matter, anybody else's priority list in your company, just tell me, and I will put this into a low-priority status. If I am reading this wrong, please tell me."

That should bump them into some sort of honest revelation. If it's a no, not now, not ever, no problem; look for an intro to somebody who you could help more and make a quick exit.

If they are in, you are well on your way.

O... Onboarding

Be Useful... Now

Before You Go

Expectations

Unique Connections

Set an Agenda

Explore Their World

Finding Time/$/Resources

Understand Who Cares

Let Them Know You

Next Steps

Onboarding

What Else Can We Do/Referrals?

The thrill of victory is so short-lived in sales. The emotional high or sense of satisfaction from receiving the signed contract, deposit money, or PO can, and perhaps should, get lost in the shuffle of the business of getting the account started.

This isn't the time to take a victory lap and celebrate. This is the time to double down on proving to your new customer that they made a great choice in hiring you and your firm.

Recently, a colleague of mine won a piece of business that had mad potential. They were well funded, a huge market, and the service he offered would certainly help them achieve their goals. Nine months later, the account was ninety days in arrears, not paying their bills, not in sync with the service provider, and were rather dismissive around all the work they had provided and how they could have capitalized on the work to their advantage.

Think of it this way: every time you get a new account or a new project from a current account, it's a chance to start anew and train them **to become the best account you have ever had.**

If they haven't worked with you before, they have no idea how to become a great account. Setting them up for success is a critical priority.

If you want to have a great relationship with anybody—your spouse, employer, employee, car wash guy, or new customer—you have to set it up right in the beginning, before you get too ingrained in the wrong behavior that gets you nowhere.

My first marriage was a challenge. Neither of us had been married. We had differing expectations and hadn't really talked about it—or even knew what to talk about—going in. I was blessed with three amazing children, and I tried to apply the lessons I learned from that marriage to my current marriage, and we have the most incredible relationship I could ever imagine.

So, back to your life.

Here are my recommendations to start off on the right foot and **train your new customer to become the best customer you have ever had:**

1. APPRECIATION

When they hire you, **show appreciation, but don't go overboard** thanking them endlessly for giving you a shot.

When they hired you, in their mind, it was a trial run, and they are hoping you're fantastic, but they are not yet convinced, nor should they be, that you will deliver as promised.

Keep it appropriately understated.

> **Don't say this:**
>
> "Donna, I can't thank you enough for hiring us. I promise we won't let you down; earning your trust is the most important thing in my life, and I can't adequately express my joy that you hired us."
>
> **Say this instead:**
>
> "Hey Donna, I appreciate the vote of confidence in bringing us in; I know you had other choices, and it matters to me personally, that you wanted to work with us."

No, don't do that. Acknowledge, show appreciation, and remember, you are about to do a bunch of work for them that may not be easy to do and will no doubt have its challenges.

2. FIX A PROBLEM

They hired you to either fix a problem that they have or improve upon their current situation. In almost every sales environment, those are the likely possibilities.

If they hired you to fix a problem that they had, I want you to consider: who owns the problem?

If you answered, "Well, I do now,"—wrong! It was their problem when they hired you; **it is still their problem or opportunity**, and it is your job to help improve their situation, but that will likely require their cooperation, participation, and perhaps even some luck.

Don't say this:

"Stewart, thanks for giving us the business; we will have this working right in no time. Just sit back; we have this under control. You're going love the new system."

Say this instead:

"Stewart, I know your computer systems have been a headache for a while now, and I can promise you that we will eventually be making things a lot better. However, you have some very complex issues, as we have discussed prior. They won't be easy to fix, and it will take some time to get this the way I know you want it to be.

"In the meantime, I need you and your team to be working with us by gathering the data we asked for, shutting down early enough in the day for us to get our work done at night, and having a lot of patience until we get it just right. Once it is just right, you're going to be super happy, but again, you have some seriously messed up technology issues."

All you are doing is asking to buy a set of problems, have your bills not paid, and end up with a bunch of angry customers who expect too much and don't want to own their part in the problem!

3. MANAGE THE EXPECTATION

Imagine you were blindfolded and walking into a strange room that was 100 feet across and filled with dangerous open electrical wire, cut glass, and some large areas of dry rot in the floor.

If you can make it across the room in less than two minutes, without incident, you can check in to the St. Regis in Bora Bora for a week, all expenses paid. You are allowed to hire one person to explain to you where to go and guide you through the room. With their help you get the prize. If they don't advise you of exactly what lies ahead, you have to turn around and buy your own ticket home, no Bora Bora resort.

Every time any customer hires you to do anything for them, use the time wisely to explain all the potential pitfalls of working with you and how to avoid them and make sure they are clear on their part in working with you to get the desired outcome you both want.

Don't shy away from telling your new customer the truth. We all know over-promising and under-delivering is the number one new client downer, yet it happens all the time, either because the client is too busy to stop and meet with you and your team or you haven't committed to a formal onboarding process that helps you really win their trust.

People trust you more when you tell them what could go wrong. You gain credibility by fearlessly leaning into the prior problems you have seen with other customers, and it's YOUR JOB to tell them the truth. If you set the tone early, you will pave the way for a great long-term, multi-repeat purchase relationship; if not, they will likely hear what they want to hear and kill you with scope creep, unpaid invoices, and bad reviews.

If you set the right tone early, they could stick with you forever, come back frequently, and become a raving fan of yours.

W... What Else Can We Do/Referrals?

Be Useful... Now

Before You Go

Expectations

Unique Connections

Set an Agenda

Explore Their World

Finding Time/$/Resources

Understand Who Cares

Let Them Know You

Next Steps

Onboarding

What Else Can We Do/Referrals?

One of my favorite questions to ask toward the end of any meeting about anything is, "What else?" In other words, what else did we miss? Anything left incomplete? What am I forgetting? Think of this as your catchall safety net for everything you may have forgotten to do along the way.

Maybe you rushed through one of the earlier components? Maybe you need to emphasize a rough spot that felt incomplete. Certainly, there are at least **two more giant things left hanging to discuss** to be complete.

Most companies I have worked with have the potential to double the size of their company or territory without ever even getting any new clients. There is often so much untapped opportunity—if we could just get to that ideal client scenario. We need to start early, like we were just discussing, as a continuation of the onboarding. There are two critical requests I suggest making right out of the gate with your new customer.

1. LOOKING AHEAD

Let's talk about where we could end up someday. Not now, but down the road, assuming their early experience with you goes very to extremely well. I think painting a picture of what a win looks like for your new customer and you could be tremendously helpful in **building the volume of future ongoing business.**

Don't say this:

"We would really like to get a crack at that fabrication business," or, "My boss is on me to get you to use us for your repair work in addition to the supplies we sell you," or, "Any chance you could let me quote you on your hard to fill jobs?" No, no, no. All that, again, sounds needy and desperate—desperation is never attractive.

Say this instead:

"Jeff, I know right now all that matters is making sure this comp plan analysis goes well, and we get a big win by rolling it out and attracting some top talent that you have been after. Assuming this goes the way you and I are both hoping it will, I'm going to want to have a more meaningful conversation about some of the other HR resources that we haven't even discussed yet. My hope is that at some point, you start feeling like it's just a lot easier to have us handle your comp, HR, and payroll. Not today, but down the road. Anything like that sound like a conversation worth having, or is that just me thinking crazy?"

Lean in here. If you have confidence in your other offerings that they have yet to experience, put them on their radar, and try to get a commitment to at least explore them at the appropriate time. If you believe it could help them, then it's worth talking about. If you are only bringing it up because your company wants you to, and you guys suck at that additional offering, then leave it in the bag and out of sight until your company gets its act together. Sorry if that hurts anybody's feelings—it's all part of the learning process.

2. REFERRALS

Last piece—I really left the best for last—wait for it...can you guess?

Referrals, referrals, referrals. My next book is really all about having the kind of relationships where all you are doing is sifting through referrals, but you may not be there yet.

I have been a student of this topic for a long time. It's my favorite way to grow. It should be yours.

Number one reason we don't get referrals: we don't ask. Come on, people, what's up with that?

You know why, don't you? Fear. Stupid nonsense we tell ourselves about not wanting to say the wrong thing at the wrong time. I get it—I am not immune to fear and have spent plenty of time in my life in my head, wondering what to say and when. The title of this book is *Conversations Made Easy* so, once again, I'm going to make this easier for you.

Don't say this:

"Here are a few of my cards that you can pass around. If you send me any customers, I will buy you dinner. We love being referred to your friends and family." Ugh, yuck, disgusting, puke!

I would like to share one more story with you about referrals first.

Years ago, a man named Paul bought a company, built it up huge inside a couple of years, sold the company, bought a large horse ranch in Montana, and retired with his family at an early age. He was in the residential roofing business. Here is how he **onboarded** new customers. He would have his onboarding meeting in the kitchen.

Say this instead:

"First of all, I wanted to let you know that I appreciate the vote of confidence in trusting us with your project; I know you had other options, and it matters to me personally that you selected us.

"I want to make sure you are aware of what's about to happen here in getting your roof replaced. It's designed as a four-day project. Barring any weird weather, which will throw the schedule way behind, we should be in and out of here inside of four days.

"Day 1, it's going to be a bit of a war zone. We are going to have a four-person crew on your roof pulling off all the old shingles; there is going to be a giant dumpster in your driveway. Every now and again, we miss the dumpster. If we damage a plant, I promise we will replace it before we leave the premises.

"By the way, it's not uncommon to get some dirt or debris falling inside the house, so if you have any important clothing, comforters, or anything else you don't want to get soiled, please take some precautions. Oh, by the way, I haven't seen a cat or any other pets, but if you have any, they won't like it either, so maybe you could arrange for them to be elsewhere for a few days?

"By the end of Day 1, I will be back on your roof with my quality control manager, and I will be personally inspecting the structure for any damage, dry rot, or termites that could undermine the stability of the roof. I want to warn you—in around one out of four jobs we do find some damage. Normally the repairs are relatively minor, meaning less than $2,500 worth of repairs.

"At the end of Day 1, I will let you know if we find anything, and normally we can still stay on schedule. By the end of Day 2, we will have completed any structural repairs.

"By Day 3, we will be installing the new roof, and by Day 4, I will be back on the roof with my quality control manager, and we will be personally inspecting every flash point, every vent, and every skylight to make sure that roof was installed exactly to code so you will never worry about rain or unplugging something and dragging out a bucket or tarp again—for as long as you live in this house. That's my job.

"Here's your job. While we are on the roof, making sure the job goes like it's supposed to, I wondered if either of you even know any of your neighbors, and if you would be open to checking with them about whether or not they might need the same kind of help.

"Are you open to that?"

That's it in a nutshell. "Are you open to that?"

> **Don't say this:**
>
> "Could you refer me to your neighbors, colleagues, friends, family?"
>
> **Say this instead:**
>
> "Would you be open to connecting me to people that you would naturally run into who need this kind of help?"

This is a case where the words matter: **"connecting us"** to others is received very differently than "referring me" to others.

We will talk more about making this a habit and then making it easier for you.

That's it—in a nutshell. If you do everything I suggested in this chapter, you should feel really good about your effort and what you have done. At this point, whatever happens, happens. Maybe they do become your next best client. Maybe they kick you out of their office? I don't know, I'm not worried about it, and you shouldn't be worried about it either.

In either case, take the lesson. Review what happened. Become a student of the game. Relook at your calls with customers, and do this:

Tell on yourself, don't beat yourself up. Let me repeat:

Tell on yourself, don't beat yourself up.

You make a mistake, forget something, or deliver it with the wrong tone, look, etc.—so what? Learn from it, grow stronger, get better, and slowly and consistently acquire some great customers who love you, buy everything only from you, and introduce you to at least two other customers per year, and you're set for life.

Don't quit before the miracle happens. If you're only in your first year in the territory or field you are in, hang in there; it's a two-year sprint uphill to get to a point where you feel like you know what you are doing.

It's a five-year journey to the top of the field, and I promise you, if you follow this, you will get there—we aren't done yet.

Please refer back to the summary of **BeUseful...Now** again and again, before and after every call.

In summary, I gave you a model to quickly connect to your customers in a very authentic, genuine way while bravely talking about all the real issues in the most relatable way possible.

Here's a reference tool to help you, which you will find at ChrisJenningsGroup.com as well.

Before You Go

Expectations

Unique Connections

Set an Agenda

Explore Their World

Finding Time/$/Resources

Understand Who Cares

Let Them Know You

Next Steps

Onboarding

What Else Can We Do/Referrals?

Next, we are moving on to the only part of sales that you can control: what you do—your actions, your routines, your habits.

PART 2

DO SOMETHING

———

When I go to the gym, which I do about three to four times per week, there are probably fifty to one hundred different exercises I could do any time I am there. Of course, I use about eight of the same pieces of equipment, and I know I need to work on diversifying my workout.

I want you to think about your work as you would a workout. Don't overthink where it is going to lead you. Think about the things you need to do to get there—wherever "there" is. In time, you will settle into a good routine that feels comfortable and reasonably enjoyable, and over time you will get really good at your routine.

Unfortunately, too many people give up and quit long before the miracle happens.

I can virtually guarantee that you will definitely hit your goals if you **find at least five activities** and commit to doing them at least 80 percent of the time with consistent frequency. If you are actually doing what I am suggesting and still are not achieving your goals, then go to Part 4 and look at the improvement section to diagnose the issue.

When I'm at the gym, I do three to four sets of about eight various exercises at around eight to fifteen reps per set—it takes me about forty-five minutes. I add three one-hour swims, three to five sixty- to ninety-minute hikes or treadmill sessions, one time per week on the bike for sixty minutes plus, and every other day abs/core. That's it. Nothing special. It's just my routine. It doesn't drain me of any energy. In fact, it energizes me. I look forward to those workouts; I don't think about whether I want to do them—I just do them. I love my routine.

I'm never going to be on the cover of *Men's Health*, but I feel really good about what I am doing for my health.

Similarly, you need to find a workout for your career that will make you feel good about what you do.

I will give you some specific activities to choose from as a part of your new workout routine, many of which you will already be doing, but perhaps not with enough frequency or efficiency to get the ultimate results you want.

Stick with them. Get good at each one of them. Fall in love with the process. Don't sweat the results, especially out of the gate. Keep doing them because you said you would do them, and the results will be amazing.

Far too many people in sales roles give up before they ever get good at doing something. Others choose to follow a very narrow path of strategies without enough variety to really accomplish what they could.

Still, others assume *it won't work for me*, or *it doesn't work in my industry*. Figure it out, and make it work. Get better at each activity. Push yourself to work through the challenges, and the results will change your life forever.

Let's get started.

TOP THREE GOALS FOR ANYBODY IN A SALES OR BUSINESS DEVELOPMENT RELATED ROLE
1. INCOME

Give yourself a target—short-term, this year's target—and keep an eye on where you are going with two- to five-year income targets. Don't evaluate your career based on year-one or year-two income. Anticipate where you could get to in two to five years.

By the way, it takes two years to know what you are doing in just about any sales job. It takes five years to reach a point where you have real momentum. Old customers come back to you. People move to other companies and reach out to you. None of that happens in your first two years. It starts happening regularly at year five. If you stick with your career for ten to twenty-five plus years, the results will be off the charts.

So maybe today, you would be stoked to make $75K to 125K, but in two to five years, that could be $250K, $500K, or more.

Get clear on where you are going, and then just focus on what you need to do today.

2. GROSS PROFIT DOLLARS

What kind of income do you need to generate for the company you work for to earn the kind of money you want to earn? By the way, even if your compensation is based on revenue, not gross profit, I want you to concentrate on how much gross profit you are generating for your company.

Companies don't need to hire salespeople to sell stuff at low prices. If that was their strategy, they could post all their prices online, eliminate your job, and let orders come in.

The only reason companies need to hire sales teams is to offer their goods and services at healthy margins, with good profits that get reinvested in their people, their inventory, and their facilities. Think how you can effectively keep your margins high, and your value to both your customers and your employer will be respected, and you will be earning at the highest level for good reasons.

3. APPOINTMENTS PER WEEK

Very few KPIs are more important than how many appointments you go on in a week. I mean face-to-face or on Zoom/Teams where you get about an hour plus to talk through what's going on for your customer or prospect and offer ideas of how you could help.

You may need to delineate between existing client appointments and new customer appointments. For most industries, five a week is a good number, but yours might be different.

You might need five new per week and five existing per week. Depending on the size of the deals, two of each might be enough. I don't know what your number is, but there is a number, and you need to own it.

No bullshit. Ask your boss and talk to other reps. Find a solid number that feels like a stretch, but an attainable stretch. Once you decide on that number, get busy about attaining your appointment number, and everything else will fall into place.

Consistently hitting this number will be the pathway to your financial and career success. Not hitting this number will leave you, and everybody around you, second-guessing if you are right for this industry, job, or company. Don't torture yourself with self-doubt.

You belong here. You are either doing the work to hit the appointment number, or you are not doing the work required to hit the appointment number. Oh yeah, **in the beginning, this is a nightmare!**

I mean a wake-up-several-times-a-night nightmare. So, do what you can. The one thing in your life or career that you have complete control over is your activity. Fall in love with your activity regimen, and everything else falls into place. Fall out of love with your activity regimen, and welcome to the miserable world of excuse-making.

WAHHH! It's my bosses' fault, it's a bad market right now, it's the pandemic, it's my family's fault, he/she got the good territory, I got stuck with a bad territory, I have cheap clients, I have stupid clients, my leads suck, we don't have a good SEO source or appointment setter— to quote Judge Judy, "I DON'T CARE!" I don't care what your excuses are. I care about what you are doing.

So let's get busy. Are you with me? If so, let's do this. If you're not, quit today, and apply for a job in operations. That isn't a bad thing at all, but you won't get to double your income every year. So, if making big steps forward in your income and results are high priorities for you, let's get busy!

The following pages are devoted to your choices for activities that will put you in conversations with your preferred audience.

A couple things I want you to know going into this section: As I have emphasized, whether or not you do the things I suggest here is totally on you. Also, don't expect to be great at any of these until you have done them hundreds or thousands of times. Don't judge your results based on the first one hundred or even one thousand at-bats. Base the results on how these work for you in years two through ten.

Also, if you have a coach who listens to how you are executing on each principle, and the coach is good, you will start to see better results after the first one hundred tries, and you won't have to wait until attempt number 32,303.

A couple other notes: try to enjoy the experience of getting to know some great new customers and other connectors along the way, and don't worry about the people who aren't ready to play.

FINDING YOUR TOP FIVE ACTIVITIES

Lastly, mix it up. If you are a relentless door knocker, great, but don't have that be your only play. Like in football, if all you do is pass the ball, it won't work as well because that can't be your only play in the playbook. At a minimum, have **five specific activities with a specified frequency per month or per week.**

1. GET CONNECTED BY REFERRAL

Getting referrals from people who know you to potential customers who don't know you is far and away the absolute best way to go.

Yes, I mean proactively bringing this up on a regular cadence with all known entities—your customers, your friends, your vendors, your past customers, your neighbors, etc.

Unfortunately, way too many of us are just afraid or uncomfortable, or unaccustomed to bringing it up in a way that doesn't feel completely awkward and/or off-putting, so we don't do it, the skill atrophies, and when we try it, we get awkward stalls and excuses.

Honestly, it's so simple; you don't have to overcomplicate this.

> **Don't say this:**
>
> "Well, Mr. Customer, I hope you know how much I love referrals. If you can ever think of somebody I could call, there is a steak dinner waiting for you."

Bribery is the last reason you should be getting referrals. I'm not saying that an after-the-fact thank you card or a small token of appreciation isn't appropriate; I am saying it shouldn't be the main reason it happens.

> **Say this instead:**
>
> "Kim, I know it's pretty early on in our working together, and my hope is that you quickly get to a point where you are super happy that you went with us on this project. By the way, if you start running into people who need this kind of help, I really count on you connecting me to some of those folks, and I wanted to make sure you were open to that?"

I have a hundred different ways to phrase that—check out our website: ChrisJenningsGroup.com or the follow-up to this book: *The*

Client Retention Matrix. Once you find a few that you relate to, run that play over and over; you will thank me for it down the road.

Early on in my career, I hosted a small gathering of about eight to ten prospects. I went through a lot of work to get that many people into my tiny conference room on the ground floor (basement) of the executive suite I was in at the time.

A guy named Stephen walked in late and sat in the back. He was wearing a nice suit, which very few people did in Orange County, even back then. He left early without filling out any of the forms so I could track him down later. I thought, *who is this guy, and what's his problem?*

An hour later, he called me and said he was enrolling two members of his team into my program. I found out later he made the call from the back of his limo. He was very successful—a bit arrogant, but super successful.

Anyway, his two people enrolled and introduced me to the rest of the team, who also enrolled. A new guy joined the company, named Stewart; he introduced me to a guy named Lonnie, and they became clients. Stewart then introduced me to a roll-up of about ten East Coast publishers, and I started working with all their companies.

Then a guy named Chris D. called and said he saw me working there and asked if I would help his new company, and so on, and so on, and so on. Just two months ago, Chris referred me to another guy named Andrew. I am not even naming all the people in this chain, but I can tell you that there is about a $3 million revenue trail that all started with one guy—Stephen W.

If I hadn't emphasized the importance to him and everyone I have ever met—letting them know how big a deal this is—I would have missed out on $3 million worth of opportunities. I don't know if this motivates you or not, but for your sake, I hope so.

2. FIND SOME SERIOUS STRATEGIC PARTNERS

Unfortunately, most salespeople, and perhaps most people, aren't really serious about doing large volumes of business. I take it for granted that if you are reading this, you are serious—or, at least, somebody you work for is serious, and you are afraid to pretend you read the book when you didn't.

Anyway, if you are going to make the kind of forward progress that you want to, and have it happen before you are being forced to withdraw from your retirement account, you have to get aligned with some other service or product providers that offer noncompetitive services, etc., but call on the same kinds of customers you do.

Let me warn you, you are going to kiss a lot of frogs here, but if you stay committed to the principle of aligning yourself with other smart, engaging, highly valued strategic partners, you can really multiply your sales effort.

All by yourself, you might dig up $1 million per year in new business, but you could add a zero and call that $10 million per year if you have a solid network of fifteen to fifty great strategic partners bringing you along for the ride.

Don't say this:

"Hey, fellow sales rep that I met at some random Chamber of Commerce event, maybe we could refer each other in from time to time. Let's stay in touch. I specialize in_____." Blah, blah, blah. The reality is 99.99 percent of these go nowhere.

Say this instead:

"Jeff, as one of my favorite customers, who I truly enjoy hanging out with, even if we weren't working together, I could use your help with a couple things:

1. "If you ever run into somebody who is stuck working with the wrong kind of _____ provider, I could really use your help knowing who those people are."
2. "I am also curious to know: who are some of the other resources you really count on beyond what we do for you?" Get an idea of their work and how closely aligned you might be. "Jeff, do me a favor, and send me and three of these people you just described an email; say something to the effect of 'Chris, has been really helpful for us with _____, thought you all should connect.'" That's it. Simple.
3. Then you contact the potential partner and give it to them straightforwardly: "Yvonne, it seems like you and I both do some work for Jeff. He said great things about you; I want to know more about what you do." Let her explain. If it lines up, go straight ahead with, "So Yvonne, I have a customer list of about _____ [number of clients], and I'm guessing you have a similar size list. Would you be interested in bringing me in as a potential resource to your clients who need help with _____, and I will do the same with you? Let's find one or two to start with and see if we can't help each other going forward. Are you interested?" She is going to say yes.

Here is your disclaimer: "Yvonne, if you are not serious about working really hard to find and keep great clients like Jeff, let's not start. I know we don't know each other well yet, but maybe, if we do this right, we can help make ourselves and our customers a lot happier with the results. Are you in? Here's what I don't want to do—meet every month for the next three years and never bring each other in anywhere. If you think there is even a chance that might happen, please save us both the trouble now, and let's not start."

If you can build one good strategic partner per month and keep that going throughout the course of your career, you are going to become really well known in the industry, and what ends up happening is you will have multiple people pointing you out to the same customer, and it won't take much effort at all for them to feel like you are the right choice for them.

3. NETWORK WITH INDUSTRY ASSOCIATIONS, LEADS GROUPS, AND OTHER SOCIETIES, CLUBS, ETC.

Maybe you have been a joiner, and maybe not. I have found that people who join one group are likely to join other groups, and if you network in one group, they will bring you to the next group.

Ideally, you will find three to four groups you can be an active participant in. You may be able to reduce the number of groups over time, but you will probably need to work a few for a while.

A couple of notes here:

Try to visit one new group a month while you are in a build mode, and see what groups resonate with you in both the type of people there and what you see as the potential return. Just because you visit a group doesn't mean you have to come back or join; shop the groups and see what they are about.

One great way is to ask your customers.

If no, "Are you aware of any?" It's quite possible your customer is not a joiner, but if they are, add on this statement: "Are there ever events where you could bring a guest? Not sure whether it would make sense for me to join, but I am super curious to learn more about your industry."

Try to attend an event with your customer; have them introduce you around if possible. If your customer is a member of that group, guess what? Maybe the other members make good customers. If it's a hotbed of potential, get super involved, join the board, emcee events, volunteer some of your company resources, etc.

There are soooo many options here. I am not really talking about *your* industry association, although in some cases, yes. I am referencing going to industry events in your respective customers' industries.

Options like:

A. **Specific target market industry events**—over the years, I have spoken at or attended events for groups like NAW (National Association of Wholesalers), state or national lumber associations, NTMA (National Tooling and Machining Association), and the list goes on forever. Go to our website at ChrisJenningsGroup.com for a link to a list of hundreds more.

B. Other **professional associations** that bring similar types of providers together are ProVisors and ACG (Association for Corporate Growth).

C. **Leads groups** can help—not always, but depending on your market, they can often be a great place to fine-tune some networking skills: BNI, LeTip, and others.

D. Advanced learning and **CEO organizations**: Vistage, TAB (The Alternative Board), Stanford MBA program, Strategic Coach— these are all dual-purpose groups; people come there for the learning and linger for the relationships they build.

E. **Collegiate alumni, charitable boards, and committees**— essentially anywhere where the concentration of members has a decent percentage of potential clients and/or potential referral sources.

F. **Chambers of commerce, social clubs, and service clubs**: Rotary, Lions Club, etc.

G. And a host of independents that probably are searchable on Google.

Find your top three to four, visit one new group a month, and see who they start to connect you to. Over time, going deep in two to three groups total should suffice, but every situation is a bit different.

When you meet somebody in the group:

Don't say this:

"Hi Julie, I want to give you my card. Do you have a health insurance provider, or are you open to getting a quote?" NO!!!!

Say this instead:

"Hello Julie, Chris. So, what brought you to the meeting tonight?" Take a sincere interest in the person. "What is it you do?" "Have you been coming to this long?" "I'm here for the first time and still trying to feel my way around here." "Has it been helpful to you? How so?"

Just ask a lot of questions, and be useful. If you could introduce them to a client or strategic partner, fine, but eventually they will respond with, "What do you do?" Then you can give them some context and see where it goes. Never force it. Let the game come to you. If you actually have something that would be helpful, offer to grab lunch, breakfast, or coffee at some other time; perhaps book it while there, but keep it really simple.

"That sounds interesting. I'd like to hear more; not sure I could help, but maybe it's worth a lunch or a coffee to explore how our paths may or may not line up?" See where it goes; if you're not too aggressive here, it should consistently get you one to two appointments per event. If that's not happening—guess what—you are not doing it right. Connect to our website for other details about alternate approaches to that conversation.

4. WEBINARS, LUNCH AND LEARNS, AND OTHER EDUCATIONAL EVENTS

Everybody in every field has a unique set of skills that, purely based on the volume of exposure to multiple clients applying your tools, products, and services, has allowed you to gain valuable knowledge that would be helpful to some audience.

These can be conducted at a client's office, via Zoom, held privately for one client, or offered to multiple clients or prospects.

The most important thing about getting started is to plan out a schedule of dates for any public events throughout the year and to have a goal or target for the number of events you would like to host privately for clients.

These can be free to the attendee or paid. There are reasons to have multiple types of events, and without a doubt, these work as a strategy.

My history coaching sales teams tells me most of you are already squirming at the thought of doing this and getting hung up on the details about what to present, how long, and who will come.

I promise you, if you build it (and execute it with relative consistency), they will come, and this will bring you clients.

Like I said, the key is to set the dates for the events, make a commitment to host them, and immediately start sharing the dates with an audience of people so you can't back out.

If it is a private event:

Say this:

"Hey Jud, I've been thinking about what you mentioned earlier regarding the security risks as you have been adding so many new team members across the world. I wondered if it might be worthwhile to have a strategy or thought session walking through some of what we see that works well vs. what has stopped working?" If they are interested, "I thought you might. What kind of time frame are you thinking?" If they say ASAP, "OK, soonest I could probably do is the last week of the month. How many team members do you think might be interested in joining?"

You always want everything to have that nice conversational flow—never salesy—always useful and on topic with what's relevant to them at that moment or looming ahead as a critical issue, even if not currently a hot topic.

If it's a public event:

Don't say this:

"My boss is asking me to sign people up for this webinar; it has all the latest ideas serving middle market companies such as yours." Double puke—hold your nose. Way too canned—just that approach alone is enough to scare people away, even if the topics were relevant.

Say this instead:

"Hey Jud, you still tinkering around with your security patches and settings in the network? Hopefully, you've made some good progress, and you're no longer thinking about it." If they respond with, "Oh no, we are always thinking about this," reply, "I kind of thought that might be the case. Not sure if you or your team would have any interest in attending a discussion on the topic as my guest?" If the answer is yes, "How are you looking on the last Wednesday of the month in either of the next two months?" Having more than one date is always helpful to avoid the "I'd like to, but I'm busy that day."

Obviously, you will couple this with some sort of social media and email campaign to get the word out. For the public settings, stay consistent at one session per month or per quarter. For the private sessions, always have your antenna up and on the lookout for this to be a great way to increase your exposure to people who know you and a safe way for people who don't know you to meet you and see what you and your company are really good at. If you don't have something impressive to share, well that's a different story, but truly, you have something good to share with some audience somewhere.

Once again, I get a lot of resistance on this. *There are already too many webinars out there, I've asked my customers, and they are not allowed to invite anybody in due to COVID or due to policy.* All of these are just a bunch of knee-jerk reactions, somewhat whiney excuses—an old story in your head that no longer serves you and needs to be replaced with a better story around this topic and perhaps every activity I am offering you.

A couple of stories: Miriam has heard me talk about this for years. She still digs her heels in on parts of it, but my gruesome persistence and amazing tendency to restate the truth, no matter how many times she has not acted upon it, has been paying off for her. A recently scheduled lunch and learn with the largest social media platform in the world led directly to some business within six weeks. I am so proud of what she has done with her business. She just told me this week that she was invited to share the same information with five new groups inside a new organization—all because she took the right action!

My friend and client Shawn B., who has heard me yack about this for over a decade, is now a convert. He is doing webinars once a month, and while it didn't start out this way, he now consistently signs up about 140 people for each one, with about a 50 percent show rate, and gets new business and ongoing clients out of every one of the events.

Don't quit before the miracle happens. You really just have to keep at it. Keep pounding the rock, sending out the invites, and looking for new attendees, and I promise you great things will come out of your efforts.

As soon as you believe these will work, you will prove yourself right!

5. THE HOT TUB RULE

If someone is close enough to you to be in the same hot tub, then strike up a conversation and find out who they are and what they are about.

I know we have a world filled with people plugged into their devices who appear to be checked out, but if you take some initiative and strike up a conversation, something unexpected could come out of this. The key is, don't act like you expect it to go somewhere; act a lot more like you don't expect it to go somewhere and let destiny, or the universe, or God take over and honor your efforts.

You are not responsible for the outcomes of these conversations, but you are responsible for initiating them. As I write this, I'm on a United flight on my way to Charlotte for a talk. There is a lady buried in her video game. I promise, before we land and deboard, I will strike up a conversation in a friendly way—not obnoxious, friendly—and then I will just see where it goes.

Honestly, I hope it goes nowhere. I'm feeling pretty satiated with the number of opportunities that I currently have, but if there is a chance that I could be of service to her, her company, her family, and her community, I feel compelled to strike up a conversation. Promise to let you know.

Don't say this:

"I see you are deep in your video game; I wish I had the time to just do that right now. I'm too busy prepping for a big presentation for a client tomorrow. I'm in sales for XYZ design; what do you do?" Ugh, death by a thousand lousy attempts.

Say this instead:

"Are you getting to go home or just getting started?" Perhaps: "Where's home? How long are you gone? I'm just traveling for work again after being 100 percent Zoom for sixteen months; not really sure how I feel about it yet?" If they are traveling for work: "What kind of work do you do?" If personal: "Visiting family?"

Don't force yourself on people, but don't miss out on the thousands of chances we have to meet people in safe settings. Sooner or later, these hot tub chats turn to what you do, and maybe something materializes, and maybe not.

My friend and client Darien has a real discipline around this. When he is out for a weekend and strikes up a conversation about his dog, running, or whatever, if it goes really well, he just says, "Hey I've enjoyed our chat. What's your cell? I'm going to text you my info, and the next time you're in town, you're out with your dog, or you need help with____, we should connect." He gets their cell, and not always, but often enough, a new connection is made that leads somewhere good.

The reality is that everything on this list works and works well. If it hasn't worked for you yet, either you're not doing it right, you're not doing it enough, or some combination thereof.

By the way, the woman sitting next to me is an artist in the middle of drawing something. Nothing ventured...

6. ATTENDING TRADE SHOWS, CONFERENCES, AND OTHER LARGE GATHERINGS, BOTH LIVE AND VIRTUAL

I live in Orange County, California, where there are about six conference centers inside a ninety-minute drive, and during normal times between those conference centers and all the numerous functions held at hotels, I bet there are no less than fifty large scale events (two hundred to twenty thousand attendees per day per event), and if you look at the global conference schedule of events available by virtual attendance—an almost unlimited number of opportunities to get connected to more prospects than you could manage in a lifetime.

Go alone, go with your strategic partners, get your company to spot you a booth, just walk the floor, or go to the networking sessions, bring your clients, have them find more prospects for you, or work the golf event (before or after).

Perhaps film yourself while at the show and give us thirty seconds of why you are there and some of the cool companies you are working with there. Check with the show and exhibitors about linking your content to their website, or just post it on LinkedIn or other appropriate platforms.

You can call the list in advance or after, if appropriate.

Just commit to the process. Some events will feel like a waste of time, your feet will hurt, and you will feel spent. Some events will be tremendous, connecting and/or reconnecting to people you would never have met otherwise and/or rekindling old relationships that fell by the wayside. Out-of-sight, out-of-mind is so true. You probably have so many former clients and prospects at a certain point that you couldn't possibly stay in touch with them all.

When you meet somebody new:

Don't say this:

"Hello Dave, (reading their badge), you were just the person I wanted to see. We have some amazing widgets with warranties far superior to our competitors, and I would really love to send you some samples for you to compare to what you are currently using." OK, I have a stomachache just listening to this pretend dialogue, let alone witnessing it live (which I have done frequently).

Say this instead:

"Dave? I'm Chris. How's the show working out for you so far? What brought you here? Still happy you came or wishing you stayed home? I'm still on the fence. Ironic that you brought up buying better widgets. Don't be shocked, but that's what I do. I'm guessing right about now you're wishing you never said hi to me." Pause. "What widgets do you currently use? Those are good, aren't they?"

Let the game come to you. Never push.

7. PUBLIC SPEAKING

In my humble opinion, there aren't many more effective ways to gain traction with an audience than finding ways to be the featured, warm-up, or backup speaker at any number of events.

This could include speaking at those trade shows or networking gatherings or having a paid-for event that you offer to the public.

You could get lined up as a TED Talk speaker; these days, it is getting easier all the time.

Start your own YouTube channel (BTW, I will be listing out social media strategies as an option to add to your activity. I will explain how I prioritized this list later).

Maybe start small by speaking at your stepdad's Rotary Club, and see if you don't get booed out of the place. Seriously, nobody will boo you out of there unless you are a self-absorbed knucklehead who needed that to happen to wake you up to the realities of how you come across.

The point is to become a subject matter expert that the world, however small or large a piece of the world you want to be known in, is willing to listen to. If you are good enough at what you do to become a widely or locally known SME (subject matter expert), then guess what—your phone will ring, and you won't have to spend your entire career calling strangers for a living. BTW, I am about to get to calling strangers; we just aren't there yet.

Keep working on refreshing your titles and topics of the talks you give. Have two to three core programs you deliver, and get really good at delivering those programs. Join Toastmasters or the NSA (National Speakers Association), hire a speaking coach, talk to other speakers about what they did and how they got started, and most importantly, have some fun with it. Use this as another reason to fall in love with your process and continue to be patient with yourself as you develop.

Tell on yourself when you screw something up, but never beat yourself up, and know we are all growing at different rates with different learnings at each stage of the process.

Build the structure of your talk around our **BeUseful...Now** process, and go talk to people, whether your audience is 1, or 1,001, treat it like a conversation, including all of your misspeaking stumbling points; it will likely make you more relatable and make people more inclined to talk to you. Please see the link at our website ChrisJenningsGroup.com for additional tips.

If you find a speaking coach who is trying to turn you into a puppet, with a canned "News at 11" style of communicating, who has you freaked out about every "let me think" or "you know," they may be the wrong coach. If "you know" comes up a hundred times as a phrase in a thirty-minute talk, perhaps it's a real issue; if you use that two to three times in a thirty-minute talk, it's probably not an issue.

We have samples of some of our favorite speakers on our website; check them out and keep learning.

8. CUSTOMER APPRECIATION EVENTS

Host an event, either live or virtual, where you invite all or some portion of your clients.

Depending on how you structure the event, you may want to limit this to your very best, cream-of-the-crop clients and include some incredible extras for them. Ideally, I would offer a combination of the following attributes:

Real business payoff. Introduce a new cost-saving tip for them, bring in a speaker or SME (subject matter expert)—this could be you, or perhaps one of your strategic partners—perhaps offer some access to amazing shipping terms for a limited period, or get creative and think of something uniquely special that they wouldn't normally receive tied to your business and/or your strategic partner.

Allow for guests. This could be their customers, other vendors, or a specific group in their company who you don't normally interact with. You want to encourage this as it not only increases your buy-in from your client but it gives you exposure to a whole new audience surrounded by a bunch of people who think you are amazing. You can even allow your customers to piggyback on your hosted event by inviting X number of their customers; it's a real multiplier of the event and effort.

Get the invites out early and have event photos to be circulated long after. As soon as you invite somebody, whether they attend or not, you start getting credit for the invite, and you want to keep the after-effect in play for as long as possible via the photos, ongoing learnings, and feel-good vibes.

Fun. This could be at a casino night, a Lakers game, a golf course, etc.

Food and beverage go a long way. Depending on your budget, make the food good; it could be appetizers only, but make them tasty appetizers, and have a variety to appeal to the health conscious and those who want to indulge—a tray of pure protein for the Keto peeps and a tray of churros for the indulgers. Cross-promote with a new restaurant or food truck—lots of good options here.

Time of day and location. If you are doing something once a quarter to once every six months, perhaps alternate the time between something during the workday, anywhere from 8:00 a.m. to 4:00 p.m., and the next one in the evening. Some people have family and other obligations that could take them out of the evening affairs but would love to do something during the workday, and vice versa.

Experiment with the length, probably not less than an hour and not more than three to four. Try to keep it convenient enough to get to or think about offering two tries of the same event with different times of day and perhaps locations. Again, you might be able to cross-promote here. If you belong to a fancy high-end gym like Lifetime Fitness, they might offer a location for free and reduced food costs.

Partner with a charity. Perhaps host the event at the local Rescue Mission, Red Cross office, or other meaningful charity. It's a great way to help them get new donors and build your ties in the community. Assuming you are following lots of my suggestions, you can afford to set the tone for being a giver and think in abundance.

I once attended such an event at the Orange County Rescue Mission. I fell so in love with the organization and the way they work with their residents to get people back on stable ground that I have never stopped donating and promoting their cause ever since, and I am forever grateful to the man who first introduced me and would work with him and refer his company as often as I can.

Offer customer awards and tokens of appreciation. Again, have some fun with it. You could have the fastest growing customer, the active learner award, the king of expedites award, and so on.

Don't sell stuff. Remember this is appreciation time, not write checks to *you* time. Handle yourself accordingly the whole way, from the invite to the goodbye at the end.

Don't say this:

"Kristin, I am trying to get people to sign up to come to our customer appreciation event. I can't thank you enough for buying so much stuff from us." You would think I am making this up, but people say stuff like this.

Say this instead:

"Hey Kristin, I wanted to give you a heads up on an event we are hosting, and I have a spot saved for you. Not sure if you are up for some tasty food and libations or an espresso bar, but even if not, I have booked an expert in _____. I remembered how that was causing some real issues for you and your team, and I thought it might be helpful for you to hear their take on how to improve this.

Any interest in attending?" When they say yes, and they will, continue with, "How do you look on the twenty-eighth from ten to twelve? If they are booked, ask, "Is the fifteenth of the following month any easier for you?"

If it turns out they can't make either, "Oh well, we tried. I promise to take copious notes on your behalf and give you the highlights. If you think there is anybody on the team who would want to attend in your place, definitely let me know. In either case, I will save you a spot for the next time we do something like this."

Even if they never come to the event, you are going to get tons of credit for making the offer, and it will set you apart. If they do attend, it's a great opportunity to get closer to them in a relaxed environment and without whatever constraints they encounter communicating with you at their place of business.

9. SOCIAL MEDIA: LINKEDIN, YOUTUBE, INSTAGRAM, AND FACEBOOK

To be clear, we are not gurus of social media; however, if you don't at least have a reasonably decent LinkedIn profile, you are kind of shooting yourself in the foot. For most of us, there is some element of social media that could influence our buyers.

It really varies heavily from industry to industry, but you must, once again, pick a lane and commit to the process. It could be as simple as dedicating one hour every Thursday, before you call it a day, to sending out targeted invites, responding to your messages, and sharing a learning video for the communities you work in.

You could devote an hour a week to each platform that applies to your audience. As we mentioned earlier, the social strategies should mirror the other activities you have selected. In other words, if you are hosting or attending a lunch and learn, a client appreciation event, or a trade show, record a sixty-second video on your phone and post it on your social platforms.

For most clients these days, I recommend that you **go deep into LinkedIn**, upgrade to LinkedIn Navigator, and use all the functionality it offers.

Then **pick a second social platform: YouTube, Twitter, TikTok, or Instagram**—whichever one is most likely to suit your customer base—and get good at those two, and call it a day. There are exceptions to that rule, but not many unless you are in a very consumer-oriented business.

Please remember how important it is to have a balanced approach to the market. Don't spend all week cyber stalking your customers, but don't ignore them if they have a presence. Try to work hard to specifically offer an assist to every customer and prospect regarding how you could help them improve their social media presence, and see if they don't respond in kind.

10. PICK UP THE PHONE

So, I bet you're surprised I waited so long to talk about using the phone. You shouldn't be. The goal of the first nine strategies is to make picking up the phone easier, ideally by warming up the call for you in advance. In a perfect world, the number of strangers you are forced to call will be limited based on all the other great work you are doing to get people to come looking for you, or at least for them to not be completely caught off guard when you do reach out.

That being said, if you haven't been around long enough to have your phone ring regularly, then you have to get comfortable reaching out to others and seeing how many doors you can open.

Four Types of Calls

I am going to categorize the calls into four different groups of calls—in the order I would suggest making them. Additionally, do everything possible to get peoples' cell phone numbers and be willing to reach out to them at work and/or on their cell.

In 1995, calling cell phones may have seemed bold. Today, if people are available, getting them on their cell is best; if they aren't, they won't pick up. Also, so many people moved their office home during the pandemic, and they may rarely be back. Your best chance of catching them will likely be their cell, even if they are in transit. Obviously, don't call their cell at 6:00 a.m. on Tuesday or anytime on Saturday or Sunday, but do get over whatever stigma you once held around this. I will be giving you a bunch of ways to work on your mindset toward this and other hang-ups that cause you to talk yourself out of doing things that are good for you.

Including remembering this:

You are only calling people to find out if you can help them. You have no interest in selling people stuff that won't improve their lives, and there is a really good chance that they don't even know you exist or perhaps forgot that you exist.

Here are the four categories of calls to make:

A. Current clients
B. Past clients
C. Past prospects
D. New prospects

Current Clients

Don't say this:

"Hey Bob, just called to see if you have anything I could do for you; anything you need?" Noooooooooooo!

Say this instead:

"Hey Bob, you buried as usual, juggling six things at once? Figured as much. We'll keep it short. Last time we talked, you told me your production line was backing up waiting for supply, and I wondered if you were already able to fix that with some additional supply sources?"

Always address the reality of their situation quickly, demonstrate you care by bringing up specific things they told you before, and get updated details as to whether or not it's still an issue. **Explore Their World**, even if you think you know their world.

Get additional clarity and get back to the **BeUseful...Now** process. Once they have given you the quick update, if there is nothing there, try to get out of their way. Before you do, see if there is anything you can give them—a referral to a strategic partner, perhaps, an inside tip on what other customers of yours are doing, or a heads up on a good hiring tip.

After that, you can always ask for a referral or connection and keep moving. Perhaps book a time for a next site visit or Zoom and keep moving. Anytime you reach out to them, if you are friendly, attentive, helpful, and not pushing your own agenda on them, they will consider it a positive connection. Then, you will be back on their mind again.

Keep the contact cycle to somewhere between every two to twelve weeks, depending on your product or service.

Past Clients

Don't say this:

"Hey, Sandy, you've been on my mind a lot. I'd really like to get you back as a client again. What do I have to do to earn your business?" This is way too forward and too out of left field.

Reset your expectations—that this is never happening, and they probably forgot who you are—but call them anyway.

Say this instead:

"Hey Sandy, you still burning the candle at both ends? Figured you might have retired by now. How long have you worked there? How much longer do you figure to stay? Assuming business is still growing and doing well?" Give them some time to talk, update you, and get connected. If they make it easy on you with some version of, "I'm glad you called. We should probably talk again about_____," then great—go back to BeUseful...Now.

If not, be ready to **set the agenda:**

"Sandy, I called for a couple of reasons."

Have something to offer them:

"I know you guys are always looking for good stainless platers, and I found one recently that has worked well for some other clients and thought I would connect you."

It must be something that you know would help them.

"Second reason, I had this lingering suspicion that you and I left on a slightly sour note"—get real with them here, and lean in to whatever may have gotten in the way of working together from before. "I know your corporate office took over buying the inventory you used to get from us, but I was mostly concerned that you felt like we let you down in some way." Odds are that wasn't the case, but if there was a problem, it allows you both to clear the air.

Then continue:

"So, on the off chance we should be reconnecting for any spot supply or last-minute orders that corporate wasn't handling, I thought I would just make sure we were on good terms."

Then, if the window is there, start **Exploring Their World**, and see where it goes.

Worst case, you end up with nothing, they remember you if they go somewhere else, and maybe you get a referral to somebody else inside their organization or outside of it. Keep growing your connections.

Past Prospects

These are the people you took a crack at and missed. You don't have to call all of them, and you don't have to call them often, but at least check in to inquire how things turned out for them and who they went with; see what you can learn, and keep the door open.

Don't say this:

"Hey, Shelly, wanted to see if you'd be willing to give us another shot; we really want to earn your business." This all sounds too needy, too desperate, and just wrong.

Say this instead:

"Hey, Shelly, I've been staring at the phone wondering if I should call you or not. Last we talked back in March, I was starting to think I rubbed you the wrong way." (Or, "I was hoping you hadn't felt like we let you down.") "I know you ended up going a different direction, hopefully with great success, and I wanted to make sure of that, and get an update on the big acquisition you were in the middle of." It's important to take responsibility for what happened in your mutual past. Odds are, again, that it wasn't really about you, but it opens the door for dialogue, which at this point, is all you could hope for.

This could pave the way to new opportunities, and if so, follow the **BeUseful…Now** process. Always follow the process. Once again, fall in love with the process, and don't get overly hung up on the results. Become a student of the game and develop your skills. While your competitors are going through the motions, not critically evaluating how they go about their process (if they even have a process), you are getting stronger with every call. It's probably an imperceptible amount from call to call, but the real goal is to get better all the time and watch your conversion rate grow.

OK. Here we go.

New Prospects

So, I have saved this activity for last. Not because it isn't important—it is. I wanted to make a point. All the other activities I have given you will make it so much easier to call people because you will have some prior connection.

In a perfect world, you will only be making a small percentage of your calls to brand new people without any context or prior history, but you have to approach it like this: if your appointment goal is ten per week, and all the other activities netted you seven appointments, then the other three need to come from calling strangers.

You will have to keep calling strangers to hit your appointment target until either (A) your appointment goals lower because your conversion rate is getting higher, or (B) you get good enough at all the other activities that this is no longer necessary to achieve your targets. However, until you get there, you are here, so let's get busy.

A couple more things to note:

First, I don't know if you are calling five strangers per day or two hundred strangers per day. The average in the world of sales is sixty-five calls per day.

Second, you are calling strangers—people you have never met before—who are probably busy either at work or home, and you are asking them to give you money for something they weren't even thinking about before you called. So, keep your expectations extraordinarily low!

Allow yourself to be pleasantly surprised when they do show interest, and commit, once again, to the process, without judgment over the outcome.

Lastly, if you are newer in your career—say in the first two to five years—this is a rite of passage, a humbling learning experience that will give way to large quantities of gratitude down the road when you no longer even have time to call strangers because you will have so many clients coming to you.

In 1995, I literally opened the yellow pages and started making calls to complete and random strangers. I was a thirty-two-year-old, brand new to sales training, and I looked no older than twenty-two. I was calling business owners, sales leaders, and other highly commissioned professionals, and I wondered if there was any chance this could possibly work.

I got a water filtration company on the line and was quickly transferred to then-Sales Manager Jed. He didn't know I had just started in the business. He didn't know that nobody had ever written me a check for any sales training, but he did tell me on the phone that he had a newer guy he was starting in sales and wanted to get him some help. I learned a little bit more. He invited me out to their office, and lo and behold, while I was there, he wrote me the very first check anybody ever wrote me for something I had just started doing that month, September 1995, in Irvine, California.

As many of us do, I saved a framed copy of that first check.

Eventually, Jed started using me for all the people on his team. Later, Jed got a financial backer and started a brand-new company, and they used me all the time for their team over the years. By a weird circumstance, I ended up training his mom, Bonnie, who worked for a different company. All this from a random cold call.

Sidenote: Jed was an intense guy. A real driver, figuratively and literally, he liked to race motorcycles, mountain bikes—probably any competition. This next part is sad but important. He was out for a random bike ride in Peter's Canyon one day, pulled over to the side of the trail, and died from a massive heart attack in his early fifties. Please get your regular checkups. This is a great life we are given, and taking care of ourselves and scheduling our own preventative maintenance tests really matters.

OK, back to the reason I'm guessing you got this book.

I did not say this:

"Hello Jed, this is Chris Jennings, and I know busy sales managers like you probably don't have time to train your team, which is where I come in, our tested methods for driving sales..." blah, blah, blah. If I had said that, Jed would have been gone in thirty seconds.

I said something like this instead:

"Hi Jed, it's Chris Jennings, and I'm pretty sure we have never met; frankly, this call is bound to seem really random, but on the off chance it's applicable, I did want to reach out to you give you a heads up on what we do, ask you a couple questions, and let you figure out if we really should be talking or not. Does that sound fair?"

He said, "OK."

I continued, "Jed, it sounds like you're the owner." He said, "No, sales manager." I said, "Cool, perfect. I work with people like yourself who have sales teams that:

1. Just don't get out on enough appointments,
2. When they do go out, they get hit with all kinds of objections around pricing, etc.,
3. They put together really detailed quotes and proposals that go nowhere, or
4. Guys like you run out of time to personally oversee every call.

Anything like this go on in your company, or is it something completely different?"

He said, "Well, most all of that is true, and I do have a new guy that could use some help."

I said, "That's interesting. Could you fill me in?"

After telling me more details about the new guy, I wanted to get an appointment scheduled while we were still on the phone. Now, there are two words that I never ever want you to use while setting a meeting or an appointment.

Do you know what the two words to never use are? "Meeting" and "appointment." You may wonder why.

Think about it. We are all so busy. We are all overloaded with too much to do. So, the last thing that your prospect will want to do is set another meeting or appointment. Odds are they will stall or ask you to email them something or call them back when they aren't so busy—all nonsense.

> **Say this instead:**
>
> "Would it make any sense to invite me over? I can find out more about what is going on with (fill in the blank) you and your sales team, you can ask me questions about what we do, and then you can decide if this would actually help or not. Does that make any sense?"
>
> If your prospect just spent the last five to fifteen minutes telling you about their problems with the issues you solve, then there is a 95 percent chance the prospect says, "Sure, that makes sense."
>
> All you do then is say, "Looking at your calendar, is there a day that works better for you over the next week or two?"

Once they give you a date, you are just scheduling the time, which I would immediately follow with an Outlook invite, and in the invite, bullet some of the important topics:

- Develop new sales guy
- Help with appointment setting
- Increase average territory monthly revenue

That's it—relatively simple. The only thing that gets in your way is you getting stuck in your own head, trying to be too smart, trying to sound ultra-professional, or getting overly giddy and weird because you are finally getting somewhere.

Let's keep it real; not every call goes like that. We do get hung up on, dismissed quickly, snarled at, blown off, etc. I don't care!!! Keep learning. Keep getting better. In the words of Phil Knight from his amazing book *Shoe Dog,* just keep going; you have to just keep going. Phil didn't just think of the swoosh, and the whole world started buying Nikes. He spent the first seventeen years in the business desperately afraid of being found out as somebody who didn't really know anything about shoes and potentially going bankrupt and ending up back at his parents' house. We all have to just keep going. Now known as: Just DO It. I'm good with either version.

A couple notes to add:

If you get a lot of cancellations, immediately after you book the time, tell them:

"Hey, I don't call to confirm appointments, so I just wanted to make sure this time works for you. If there is even a chance that you're going to be calling early that morning asking to move it around, postpone, etc., then could we just pick a different time now?"

Even if you were able to **Understand Who Cares**, make sure to ask:

"Is there anybody who is going to feel left out if we don't include them? Anybody going to get their feelings hurt if they are not invited?"

Get a few details and decide if they belong in the room. General rule of thumb: if they are at an equivalent level of authority or higher in the organization, get them on the invite.

If they are a level down in authority or lower, perhaps better to have them around and available if necessary. If you sell shipping, you want the owner, CFO, or VP of ops. You probably don't want the accounts payable person who doesn't want to bother setting up a new vendor or the shipping manager that allows the overpriced, poor service-oriented vendor to keep failing to deliver on time because they set up the shipping manager with Lakers tix.

So that's it. These are all the activities you need to choose from.

Do us both a favor and, right now, while this is fresh, grab a piece of paper or download from our website our **30 Minute Success Plan** and take no more than the next thirty minutes to write out an action plan committing to your top five activities—each one having a specific frequency over a period of time.

Name: _____

30 Minute Success Plan

GOALS

Income $:	_____	**Per year**
Sales/GP$:	_____	**Per month**
Appointments:	_____	**Per week**

	Action Plan	Goal per
1)		
2)		
3)		
4)		
5)		
6)		
7)		
8)		
9)		
10)		

Which could be:

My top three goals:

1. Income: $150K per year
2. Revenue: $120K per month in gross profit
3. Five new appointments per week with two existing customer visits

My top activities:

1. Get referrals—three per week
2. Interview one new strategic partner per week, and meet with my top five to ten monthly
3. Host one webinar or lunch and learn per month with at least ten to fifty people per session
4. Call five past clients per week
5. Call twenty-five new clients per week
6. One Hot Tub Rule per day

CHRIS
JENNINGS
GROUP
SALES, LEADERSHIP, & CLIENT RETENTION

Name: _____

30 Minute Success Plan

GOALS

Income $:	125K	**Per year**
Sales/GP$:	100K	**Per month**
Appointments:	10	**Per week**

	Action Plan	**Goal per**
1)	Generate new referrals	3/wk
2)	Calls to prospective referral sources	3/day
3)	Calls to customers completed yesterday	10/day
4)	Evaluations (Onsite/Virtual)	2/day
5)	RFQ and quote follow up	5/day
6)	Strategic partner calls/visits	5/month
7)	Networking groups	1/wk
8)		
9)		
10)		

That sums up the "what" you need to do. There, of course, will be ongoing twists and turns, edits, and adjustments. The twenty-five new calls per week may turn out to be not nearly enough, and you will have to do twenty-five per day to meet your goals.

This whole book is written with the desire to help you achieve your goals. I am not sharing in this document anything that I haven't done myself and coached thousands of others to do.

I will let you in on a secret. Everything listed here works. Everything. Now you may not believe that yet, which I am about to deal with, and you will not be at the top of your game out of the gate. As I mentioned, it will take time to get where you want.

When I was $127K in the hole, leveraged mostly on credit cards with three small kids under the age of eight counting on me, it seemed like an incredibly tough journey, and I was desperately scared and often stayed up late watching the movie *Alive* and eating ice cream to drown my sorrows. Creditors called my house multiple times a day, and I answered and honestly told them that I couldn't pay them yet, but I would call them back and arrange a schedule.

I was upside down in the home I lived in—in a gated neighborhood for God's sake! While it seemed like everybody around me was getting rich after getting hired by pre-IPO companies, I channeled my fear into faith. Yes, faith in God and faith in my willingness to do the work required to find enough clients to earn enough money to support me and my family.

Here was my actual 30 Minute Success Plan at the time.

Top three goals:

1. Income: $150K per year
2. Revenue needed to make that: $25K per month
3. Appointments per week: ten total, eight new prospects

Top five activities:

1. Five referrals per week
2. Three networking meetings per week
3. One speaking event per month (at an association, etc.)
4. One lunch and learn every three weeks with twelve people in attendance
5. One Hot Tub Rule conversation per day
6. One strategic partner meeting per week (this took forever to make it good, but when it hit, it changed my life)
7. One hundred fax blasts per week (email was brand new at the time)
8. One customer appreciation event per quarter
9. Seventy-five calls per week
10. Call all clients once every two to four weeks

Yup, it was more like ten separate things, but no matter what, I got to about six to eight of them every week. I tend to set higher goals to stretch myself, but many people prefer to set more achievable goals and hit them with consistency to avoid depression, ice cream, or watching movies where people are worse off than I am. BTW *Alive*—it's a spiritual movie in my mind.

OK, one final thing in this chapter to complete the activity section.

In the 1990s and well into the 2000s, I regularly attended several different types of networking groups. This guy named Barry had something where we met every week, I think Fridays at 7:00 a.m., and mingled. One of us usually spoke about some topic related to our business, we passed around cards, and we desperately tried to sell each other our various goods and services.

I met a woman there, whose name I can't remember, but she was older than I was, a consultant of some sort. I must have been whining a little bit about trying to fit it all in, and she asked me a question that shaped my life going forward forever.

"Do you have an ideal week?" "No, I don't think so; what is that?" I responded. She continued, "It's the week written out in an ideal scenario of how you would like to spend your time each day." *Good idea*, I thought.

I mean, my life was, at the time, completely out of control, going broke, caring for young children who all had sleep issues (guessing that was the parents' fault by now, but what did we know), when I wasn't getting my five hours a night (not enough BTW), I was with the kids, working, or doing my activities to the best of my ability.

So the idea of creating an ideal week, to me, was inspiring—working toward a future that I was not living at that moment, but hoping to set the wheels in motion to make my future better than my present.

Part of what separates human beings from the animals is the ability to look into the future and plan for a better existence than we are living at that moment. It's a psychological concept called "perspection," and apparently, less than 10 percent of human beings take advantage of this amazing ability. Most just go along with the flow of life, accepting their current situation as the way it has to be going forward.

Yes, today you might be making sixty-five calls a day, getting hung up on 90 percent of the time, working eighty hours per week, with no vacation, making only $36K per year.

However, tomorrow, if you can imagine it, put it on paper, or a spreadsheet, or a Google Doc, or however you do things, you could be making fifteen calls per day, working only four days a week, taking four weeks a year off, making over $400K per year. You just need to commit to the process.

Write it out. All seven days, all 168 hours, from the time you get up to the time you go to bed. How do you wish to spend your life? If it's important, it goes on your ideal week. You may not be there today, but this is a bit of, "If you build it, they will come."

Script it out, do the activity, fall in love with the process, and dream big.

Here is a sample ideal week. I have been following a similar one for years.

Ideal Calendar

Time	Sunday	Monday	Tuesday	Wednesday	Thursday	Friday	Saturday
6:00		Health		Health		Health	
:30		Workout		Workout		Workout	
7:00			Elevate	Networking	Elevate	Accountablity	
:30						Club	
8:00	Personal Time	Phone Prospect					Email
:30		A List	Client Portfolio Dev		Client Portfolio Dev		Paperwork
9:00		Email	Client Portfolio Dev		Client Portfolio Dev	Calls	Expenses
:30		Calls for events	Appointment	Appointment	Appointment	Calls	
10:00		Calls for events	New	New	Calls for events	Email	Personal Time
:30		Calls for events	Email		New	Appointment	
11:00	Family/Friend					New	
:30		Appointment					
12:00		New	LNL/Zoominar	LNL/Zoominar	LNL/Zoominar		
:30			LNL/Zoominar	LNL/Zoominar	LNL/Zoominar	Phone Prospect	
1:00							
:30							
2:00			Client Portfolio Dev	Phone Prospect	Phone Prospect	Referrals	Family/Friend
:30		Team Mtg	Client Portfolio Dev	A List	A List		
3:00			Appointment	Leads	Email	Paperwork	
:30			New	Paperwork		Expenses	
4:00			Paperwork	Expenses		Expenses	
:30				Email		Prep for week	
5:00		Networking					
:30							
6:00							
:30							Church
7:00	Prep for week	Family/Friend	Family/Friend	Family/Friend	Family/Friend	Family/Friend	
:30							
8:00							
:30							
9:00							
:30							

All you need now is to further visualize the future and share those hopes and dreams with yourself, your creator, and all those you hold near and dear.

GOAL BOARDS

Goal boards, a.k.a. vision boards, a.k.a. dream boards are basically just a pictorial representation of how you would like your life to unfold, both in the short term and in the long term.

I love these for all people. Sales folks, business owners, and professionals, and I especially love them for families.

I have always had my kids creating goal boards since about the age of eight-ish. They got $50 per year to show me a picture of their goal board and explain to me what was on there. Normally, I have people get a hold of a bunch of magazines, cut out the photos, and paste them onto a large white piece of cardboard.

More and more, I see people download the photos and create a virtual board that is used as a screensaver or other such purpose.

One year one of my kids drew out pictures of all her goals. She had ten things on the sheet of paper, and later in the year, she had to remind me that she had accomplished all of the goals she set out to accomplish that year.

One year, at a graduation brunch, I reminded some of my now-adult kids that I hadn't seen any goal boards from them yet that year and that the deal still stood. Our goddaughter, Hailey, said, "What's a goal board?" We explained and, thus, started our habit of expanding the offer to all the kids we met through our friends, etc.

To me, it's a great habit to teach young people that you can accomplish whatever you set your mind to, and if you don't set your mind to something, you will get roped into other people's plans for you, so why not accomplish what it is that you want to accomplish and paint the picture of your ideal future.

Earlier, I referenced "perspection," which, again, really just identifies the unique ability of human beings to think of a better future and work toward it materializing.

In the animal kingdom, the animals are purely reactionary. What is happening right now is all there is.

As human beings, we have the ability to work toward creating better futures. I have highlighted exactly how to create a plan of action that will help you create your ideal future. Just because things don't materialize exactly at the schedule that you hoped they would, don't give up. Never give up. Don't quit before the miracle happens.

I know many may be skeptical that this idea has any merit. But for the sake of argument, what harm is there in believing in your future? If you create the picture of the car you want to drive, the home you want to live in, the income you wish to earn, and the charities you wish to support, why not do that?

You start enjoying your vacation as soon as you book it, so why wouldn't you start booking your future?

It may be a year out, five years, ten years—we really don't know.

But as long as you are willing to do the work, why wouldn't you paint the cherry on top and visualize your future?

I did mention before that certain types of goal-setters prefer to set more modest goals, and that's fine too.

Put a two-bedroom condo on your goal board for starters, and take it from there.

Some of the things on your goal board are free—helping another; a walk on the beach, at the lake, or in the forest; free time; or watching reruns of *Friends* with your friends and family.

Please take time to create what you want now, and then just do the footwork, and let's see where the results fall. No exact timeline, just process, action, dreams, and results—rinse and repeat.

Take a look at a sample goal board of mine that I created after my divorce in 2001. I knew, at some point, I would end up in a relationship again, and there is a photo of a woman with her back to me in a pool. Can you see it?

Now, look at the photo of my wife, Lenna, on our honeymoon.

One of my dear friends and mentor, Les Whitney, and his wife, Teresa, often take actual photos of their goals as they are realized and paste the actual photo over the goal board photo.

This really is the good stuff.

Hopefully, that section wasn't too mushy for you, and get ready for some more mushiness. It's time to write your own headlines.

PART 3

WRITING YOUR OWN STORY

———

A friend of mine was a kid growing up in Connecticut with a father who rode the train every day to work in NYC; I am pretty sure our seventh-grade classmates would have ridiculed me for talking about this next bit of content, and his dad would have dismissed it as some sort of "California Hippie Shit."

The funny thing was his father was the one responsible for driving into him the belief that he could make some decent dough in his career. Here was his father's line of reasoning:

My friend's grandfather had worked as a shoe salesman at some department store in New York, making about $10K to $20K per year. My friend's dad had a respectable job as an account manager for an ad agency in NYC, and he earned somewhere around $100K per year by the end of his career. So to his reasoning, his son should be able to make $500K per year. Now in the 1970s, $500K per year sounded like an insane amount of money, and by many standards, it still is.

So guess what—this "California Hippie Shit" does work. He always just believed that he deserved to and could find a way to make about $500K per year, which is pretty close to what he was making by his forties.

Yup, he spent some years really struggling, where he didn't get anywhere close to that, but he also had some really strong years, and he expects to make at least that much into his retirement.

So programming his headline news story to lead with "I just closed the year at about $500K in income," feels completely normal to him at this point. He is not super proud or ashamed of it; it just is what it is. His story.

Let's look at this from a couple of different perspectives:

1. HEADLINES

What are your headlines? What are the stories that you tell yourself about yourself?

If you tell yourself that you're a good mother or father, a dependable friend, a friend to God and those less fortunate, then you probably are.

Here is the problem that I see most commonly. Somebody, at some point in your life, filled your head with a bunch of nonsense about how lazy, undependable, fat, or stupid you are or that you are never going to amount to anything.

If this occurred, and you remember those moments, I am sorry if this is causing you any pain to dredge some of this stuff up, but there is a solution here.

As adults, whatever self-limiting beliefs, whatever lousy headlines we have been carrying around, we now have the power to write new stories about our lives. New beliefs about the people we have become or are becoming.

For some of us, it is absolutely time to break the mold. Whatever nonsense, old useless self-limiting nonsense, you have been holding on to, it really is time to throw out the trash. Write yourself a new story and make **that** the headline that repeats over and over again.

Sure, we all do stupid things and have off days—or weeks—where we aren't as productive as we would like, but that doesn't have to be a life sentence to mediocrity following the herd.

Quite the contrary. If you are reading this book, perhaps there is a bit of divine intervention going on. Perhaps this was meant to be—that you would choose this moment to start to leave behind all the self-limitations that were placed upon you by some influential parent, grandparent, early teacher, boss, or significant other and stop beating yourself up for whatever existed in your past and start to create a new future.

A new future where the headlines predict positive occurrences in your life. This is the second part of this, where you need to do some more work and write out what you want to carry in your head.

2. WRITE YOUR STORY

It's time to write your own story, your own headlines filled with everything you have ever wanted to occur in your life.

This isn't some Utopic Shangri-La where every day is sunny. This is your decision to take responsibility for your thoughts and program the beliefs that you want blaring loudest in your mind. Maybe you have never written out affirmations; only a small percentage of the population does.

Remember, "perspection" is your ability to think of a better future and work toward it. It's a real thing. Only 10 percent of the world actually does this, which to me, sounds crazy. If I told you all you had to do was to write down a list of new beliefs, new ways of seeing yourself and how you interact with others, and that this simple action, along with a set of already discussed activities, would lead you to a life never before imagined, why wouldn't you at least try it?

What have you got to lose? If you want to go back to your old way of thinking, your old way of performing, your old income, and blaming the world around you for your lack of accomplishments, you can always go back.

But holy shit, if it's even possible that what I am suggesting here is true, and this really works, then why not try some "California Hippie Shit" and see if it doesn't bring you some of what you want? The fact that I feel compelled to even have to argue this point is a bit ridiculous; for the record, I am not writing this book to line my pockets—odds are if I do make any money from this book, at least half of it will go to improving the lives of others, not mine: charities, employees, family, etc.

Here's how I started. Try it.

Get out some three-by-five-inch cards and write yourself five personal stories that you would like to hold as true and five business-related stories that you would like to see materialize.

Personal headlines and new story examples:

- I am a confident person who other people want to be around.
- I am becoming very healthy, filling my body with great foods and athletic pursuits.
- I am spiritually fit and at peace with my God and the world around me.
- I am a great loving husband and father who my family can count on.
- I am a friend to all dogs.

You don't have to limit yourself to five, but please try to get five meaningful affirmations that describe how you would like your life to be or that describe you moving in that direction. Please leave out any negative statements. For example, instead of "I'm going to try not to swear anymore," say, "I really enjoy using language that everybody likes hearing." Describe your future state in the affirmative.

Business headlines that are sure to help any salesperson:

- I like getting to talk to new prospects.
- There are so many great prospects out there who need my help.
- I am enjoying making $200K per year and saving at least $20K per year toward my future.
- I am getting so much better at asking for and receiving referrals.
- I deserve to be at the top of my industry, making over $250K per year, and taking at least four weeks off with my family.

All this stuff was put on paper years ago by Napoleon Hill. If you read his book from the 1930s, *Think and Grow Rich*, it says everything that I am saying. Once again, proving there are few, if any, original thoughts left. I have read that book several times, about once a decade. One of the suggestions in there is to write down a really big goal for you for way out in the future, and perhaps read it every day until it becomes true, sort of like the comedian Jim Carrey did when he wrote himself a check for $10 million and carried it in his wallet until he could actually cash the check. For a guy who grew up poor, even living in a van with his family for a while, that was a big leap, especially starting out in stand-up comedy. Come on, at least in sales, people expect you to make money.

Anyway, I had written down one of those big goals and tucked it away in my nightstand at my home on 3 Heather in Irvine, California. Some years later, when I was cleaning out the drawer to move to my new home, I came across the card, and—you guessed it—everything had come true.

Like I said before, you need to back this stuff up by actually doing the activity. Thinking you are thin while still eating four bowls of Lucky Charms a day and never exercising isn't going to get you a cut set of abs.

So, do the work—the work of programming your mind for the desired future.

Surround yourself with people who share similar hopes and dreams. Involve your family in the adventure, tell your friends, hire a coach or a mentor, or several coaches and mentors who have been on the journey and can share with you every shortcut.

Monkey see, monkey do; just choose the right monkey.

If you don't hold your boss up as the kind of individual you aspire to be, don't let that person get in the way of your goals.

As the Harvard Law professor told Elle Woods in the movie *Legally Blonde*, "If you're going to let one stupid prick ruin your life, then you are not the girl I thought you were."

So, that sums up a lot of what you as an individual producer need to know and do. The next two parts of this book are devoted to sales leaders, and what they should be doing to get optimal performance out of their team. If you don't work for somebody who is going to read this book and implement what I suggest, then guess what—you have to keep reading and do it all yourself, and/or find a performance coach that is going to make you do it. Either way, you won't get all the way there without the next pieces.

PART 4

TEN SYSTEMS TO BUILD A GREAT PLAYBOOK

———

If you are looking for the ultimate strategy for focusing on building the skills of you and your team, just implement each of the following ten systems, and guaranteed, you will see an increase in pipeline, conversion rates, and overall profitability.

Please note that while all the examples I use in this section are related to developing sales teams, these systems could be modified to help in elevating the skills of any QA team, production team, or recruiting team in any category of business or other group environment.

Every leader has a desire to hit goals and win championships. Unfortunately, all too often, the discipline required to get your team playing at the highest level gets lost in the myriad of details that overwhelm the leaders, and most of the team suffers as a result.

This section is devoted to any individual producer, team leader, or business owner who often wonders why they or their team don't perform at the highest level.

I am in no way suggesting that the average sales leader doesn't work hard; I think they do, but I think most end up losing focus on how to increase both the quantity and the quality of the individual contributor's performance.

I can promise you this: if you fully implement what I am sharing in this book, 100 percent you will have improved results. It won't be easy. The hard thing to do and the right thing to do are usually the same.

THE TEN SYSTEMS TO IMPROVE SALES PERFORMANCE

I encourage you and anybody who you have recommended this book to start off this section with an open-minded assessment (available at ChrisJenningsGroup.com) of how well you have understood and actually implemented each one of these systems on a scale of one to ten. One meaning, you hadn't thought of it or done it; I am still giving you one point because at least you now have an awareness that the concept exists. Awareness of the problem is always the beginning of any solution-oriented endeavor.

Mark yourself or your company a ten if you are already fully aware of the concept and are consistently performing as described on a weekly or monthly basis. Remember, this is a baseline for performance enhancement, so starting out with an inflated score won't do you a lot of good, other than you are temporarily making yourself feel better about your effort.

I strongly suggest that multiple people in your organization complete the ratings independently of one another and compare notes later. Call us if you want to settle any internal disputes.

Lastly, this, and just about everything in this book, ends up in your company's playbook. If there isn't one being used today, you will have a template with all the necessary components. Don't be surprised if there isn't a ton of new stuff you have never heard of before. What most of our clients tell us is that we have organized all the pieces in an easy-to-follow manner. The difficulty is always in the implementation.

Let's roll.

SYSTEM #1: GO LIVE

Go Live is a measure of live dialogue that you and your team have with your prospects and customers. It's a phone call, a Zoom meeting, a face-to-face meeting, a factory tour, a lunch and learn—if there is live dialogue with an active or prospective customer, it counts.

The worst thing that has happened to all too many people is that they have defaulted to email as the primary and almost sole interaction with customers. Too many people today look at an email dialogue as identical to a live dialogue, and I am here to remind you that it is a completely different experience.

I couldn't care less how old you are, and yes, I understand that a lot of your customers will tell you that they prefer to communicate via email, and yes, I know how hard it is to arrange live dialogues with anybody—even people who you really want to speak with. Once again, the hard thing to do and the right thing to do are just about always the same.

Of course, we are still going to use email, texting, and LinkedIn, but they are all really methods to help create more live dialogue, not really intended to complete a transaction, nor does it demonstrate that you truly care about the prospects you are calling on.

I mentioned earlier that if you don't truly care, you need to get out of the business and do something else. Personally, I have always enjoyed talking with prospects and customers. I find their stories interesting and unique, and I want to hear what they have to say. They may or may not care what I have to say when I first speak to them, but most of the time, we are talking about topics that matter to them, and they have opinions that need to be heard. Perhaps we do have some offerings that will improve their lives, which is always a conversation worth having.

Here is how I measure whether a live conversation is better or not. If you have a customer that you email, they ask you for a quote, and you get the order 90 percent of the time at the margins you were shooting for, then keep doing that. As I said, I'm for anything that works; it doesn't matter to me who thought of it. I just want it to work.

If you are not having those kinds of results overall or with a particular customer, then you need to **Go Live**.

My experience tells me that the average full-time salesperson is only **Going Live** about forty-five minutes to an hour per day, and in most cases, that won't cut it. Maybe if you are in a seller or doer role, where you are 100 percent responsible for selling and delivering all the work, but the odds are that is not enough.

Four hours per day is the target I set for all high-producing salespeople. Anytime I have coached somebody who was consistently getting four hours per day, not only were they hitting their goals, they were blowing their goals out of the water.

It will take some serious focus on your activity and what you are doing with your time. If your ideal week doesn't call for at least four hours a day of **Go Live** dialogue, then we already know you aren't going to hit it.

Now, maybe your mind went right to the excuse journey. *I have a very remote territory, my customers don't want to see me, I tried before and couldn't get enough people on the phone, I'm too busy with paperwork and admin*—go ahead, add one to the list if you like, but remember, you have a decision to make.

Do you want to tell yourself a story that creates and supports a lack of performance, or would you prefer to go to town and start making some real money in your career, outperforming everybody in your field?

If so, you must be committed to the four hours per day.

I actually think that post-pandemic it got easier to hit, not harder. How many customers could you get to turn on their camera for a Zoom call in 2019? These days, it's common practice. If you have a geographically spread-out territory, you can hit four states in a day and still be home for dinner and a bedtime story with your kids.

Get on board with this concept and watch your life change. If you're a team leader, work with your team diligently to increase this amazing KPI, and watch the results take off. I will tell you right now, get the **Go Live** hours to an average of four hours per day, and that alone fixes a lot of sales deficiencies.

This also leads to higher margins. If you are getting four hours per day **Go Live** dialogue, you have a lot of opportunities in your pipeline, allowing you to focus on the best deals, with the highest margins, that fit what your company does best.

If you are only getting forty-five minutes to an hour per day, there is a lot less in the pipeline, and any deal quoted, even if it is a junkie deal, gets forced through your quoting process, taking up valuable quoting resources, and distracting you away from having better customers.

This will be a worthwhile effort with tremendous ongoing payoff. Get on it.

SYSTEM #2: SPECIAL TEAMS

The **Special Teams** players are all those smart, hardworking, industry experts that **Go Live** with your customers and prospects, but are not titled sales, or BizDev. They are your project managers, drivers, installers, technical resources, product managers, engineers, customer services, and accounting people.

Often, they are the people that your customers most want to interact with, but all too often, they are kept away or shy away from direct customer contact.

Think of it like this, the salesperson is, or should be, the quarterback on the account. The quarterback's job is to best utilize the team's resources, assess the challenges and opportunities, and then get the ball to them to help score more points and help the team win.

If you are not currently fully utilizing the **Special Teams** resources to their fullest, then I already know you are underperforming versus your potential. No salesperson will ever fully achieve their greatest accomplishments without a well-coordinated effort from the **Special Teams** groups.

Lots of salespeople get this kind of backward in their heads. "I own the account. I don't want anybody talking to the account but me; this account is too important." Here's the problem with that thinking: you end up handcuffing yourself to a smaller account base than you could manage, often doing less business with that individual company because you're trying to do it all. Unfortunately, you become a glorified project manager, and you are probably pissing off the project management team, which is actually good at doing that kind of work.

To me, this is a leadership issue—appropriately coordinating the company's resources and getting the maximum results from the team as it exists today.

I also know that most company leaders at some point have suggested to the whole company that "everybody is in sales," and while most of your people will politely nod as you make that assertion, under their breath, walking away from that gathering, it's, "No, I am not, that is so-and-so's job to do sales, I don't get paid to do that, and I don't have any interest in turning into some kind of used car salesperson." (Not what we asked for, but not an uncommon response.)

Let me give you an example. I was working with a steel distribution firm based in Southern California, which is where I live; most of our assignments are based in the US and Canada.

We were working with the outside sales team that was in our ear about price competition and how tough it was to win business. Often, they were at the mercy of a purchasing department that wanted to control the relationship, sometimes being the exclusive contact. Problem!!!!

We decided to do a project with the drivers. We went to the drivers and said, every time you make a delivery, we want you to find two people at each location and ask them questions from a short list.

Questions like:

- What's causing your backlog these days?
- Do you have room to inventory that much product here on site?
- Do you heat treat that before you install it?

Relevant questions that demonstrate an interest on the driver's part as to how the customer is experiencing life at their work. Here's what we found: the drivers started to come back with all sorts of interesting opportunities. When I say interesting opportunities, I mean high-margin opportunities.

If you sell a piece of steel through distribution, you might get twenty-five to thirty points of margin; if you heat-treat a piece of steel and then sell it through distribution, you might be at fifty to seventy points of margin, and you are further connecting yourself to the customer.

We all have favorite providers based on a driver, waitress, or technician that we like and trust. We just need to be intentional about those relationships and build them appropriately over time.

I worked with a large seafood distributor at one point who sold to restaurants and hotels. The president of the company commented that the sales team never gets to look in the freezer. The drivers get much better access to information in the freezer, and if the play is well coordinated, it can make a huge difference.

By the way, I also love this as a development strategy. The president I was referencing started at the company as a driver, became a salesperson, became a sales manager, became the VP of sales, and then president of the company. If you can home-grow your sales team, your odds of success are extraordinarily higher.

One of our clients tracked their success home growing the sales team and found a five-to-one payoff by promoting from the **Special Teams'** ranks to the sales team. If they hired an outside salesperson, their average first-year revenue was $300K; when they promoted from within the **Special Teams**, their average first-year revenue was $1.5 million.

A couple of additional ideas here:

1. Recognize the contributions of the **Special Teams** players with public announcements and short-term rewards, but don't expect them to be purely motivated by a financial payoff.
2. Do report back to them with wins or lessons learned from any opportunity they create or assist in.
3. I'm not always a fan of commissioning them; it can create some unintended consequences that lead to competition with the sales team, and we want cooperation.
4. Help the **Special Teams** players make this part of their job easier.

Focus on the following—specific to every customer-facing role in the company. Try to identify:

1. What will be the easiest conversations to have or questions to ask the customer? If you make it too difficult, nobody will do it. If we had asked the drivers to start knocking on doors in the neighborhood where they made deliveries, we would have gotten a flat-out rejection, and it would have killed the spirit of the project. Think line of sight; what do the **Special Teams'** players see that perhaps the sales team doesn't always see? That will stimulate interesting questions.

2. Create ways to facilitate a conversation that can be brought up naturally. Our drivers saw a lot of steel lying around a yard, and it was easy to bring up inventory management. Once again, if you make it too difficult, they won't do it.

3. What would be most helpful to your customers if the **Special Teams'** player raised the issue? Finding out that we heat-treat steel and could deliver it heat-treated, plated, etc., saved time and allowed our customers to hit their deadlines with their customers.

Think win-win-win. Not just promoting stuff that moves slowly. Think about how to make everybody's job easier, and the answers will appear.

In time, you will develop a great partnership between sales and operations. With a lot less finger pointing and blaming going on, everybody will be more efficient and more profitable.

SYSTEM #3: INSTALL A CALL RECORDING SYSTEM

I remember years ago, going to a Radio Shack near where I lived at the time and buying a small device that plugged into the phone to allow me to record calls so I could play them back for my then-coach and get feedback. Years earlier, out of college, working for a behemoth-sized company, they had groups of us flown into their headquarters to video record our presentations and give us various forms of feedback.

You have all heard the message thousands of times because every major corporation in the world does this. "We regularly record our calls for quality and training purposes." So, if you or your organization is not doing this, it is costing you money. Lots of it.

Sales is not just a numbers game. Yes, there are a lot of numbers in sales that do matter, but blindly making call after call, going on one Zoom meeting after another and not really getting any critical feedback about the good, the bad, and the ugly from a respected on-looker is a huge miss.

To me, it's unimaginable that a true sales professional may have never once listened to themselves on a recorded call or seen themselves on video.

If you are going to play the game at the highest level, then you must become a student of the game. The point of getting four hours per day, day in, day out of **Go Live** dialogue is to learn from the conversations that you have been having so that the $1 million in revenue can turn into $4 million in revenue, or $8 million in revenue, without having to work yourself into an early grave or miss your kid's entire childhood due to working too much.

The point is to get a little bit better every day, with every call, than you used to be, so that early enough in your career, you can start to experience some of the payoffs of committing to becoming a student of the game.

Now, if you are in a leadership role, these are not going to be popular suggestions. If you decide to do this, no one in your company is going to come to you and say, "This is great news! I have always wanted to work for a company where my calls could get recorded, and I could sit in a room with my boss and listen to them together." That's just not happening. But this will change performance like nothing else will.

If you aren't doing this, the odds of you catching all the nuanced areas where there is room for improvement are slim to none.

Tom Brady watches film all the time. LeBron James won the championship with Cleveland as a direct result of studying the film and making an adjustment to come back and win three games in a row against a crazy good Golden State Warriors team. Countless players, coaches, and other competitive athletes have made a career out of studying their performance in the game and course correcting at a later opportunity. Why are we any different? If you are not willing to do this, to at least make a start, you are conceding a lot of lost revenue before the game is even played.

Now, if you are the sales leader, owner, etc., you don't need to personally monitor every call, just get a sampling. Maybe get your team interested in auditing their own calls and bringing you the highlight reel.

Technology has made this so much easier. Most CRMs have a cool interface with most of the VOIP calling platforms. There are AI (artificial intelligence) tools available to screen for trends and help automate some of the coaching. This is an insanely productive exercise that only a very small percentage of people use. To me, this reeks of opportunity. If nobody in your industry is doing this, think about how much better your people can get by doing this.

Think of how much more efficient you can get as a producer, rather than working sixty-five hours a week to make $100K annually. Your goal should be getting so good that you work fifty-five hours per week and make $200K per year, or forty-five hours per week and make $400K per year.

How much time, money, and energy are you investing in getting better? Stephen Covey referenced "sharpening the saw." Are you sawing away with a dull blade or, even worse, with a broken blade, and don't know it?

If you can only get a few people in your company to commit to this, then start. Set an example and grow. It could start you on the ride of your life. If you are leading a team, they will be forever indebted to you for the forward progress they made while working for you. This is what championship teams do.

No excuses.

SYSTEM #4: WEEKLY SALES PRACTICE

I used to call this a weekly sales meeting, but frankly, there is a negative connotation with having more meetings, and I couldn't agree more that meeting for the sake of meeting frustrates everybody.

This is really designed to be run like a practice, where the individual running the practice has drills prepared to help the team improve upon their skills in any specific area of focus.

Run this like any sports team runs a practice. Everybody is going to sweat. You will get put on the spot, and you will leave that session better prepared to face the competitive circumstances that you naturally encounter in the marketplace.

One idea is to ask the team to bring one recorded call.

The first week of the month could be examples where you ran the play as designed. You brought up a new product offering, and the prospect took you up on it. The team needs to hear that call.

The second week of the month could be a common challenge you are running into. The customer wants a competitive quote or is asking for a discount. The team needs to hear live examples of price negotiations on a regular basis to be better prepared to field those requests as they come up. Most people get super anxious over this exchange and respond with some version of, "Let me see what I can do"—as I said earlier, this is a problem. The team needs to drill this in practice.

In fact, every week of the year could be devoted to capturing business at higher margins, and it would be a worthy cause.

The key point is the leader needs to be prepared in advance with meaningful exercises that help every member of the team improve their skills. You can't show up and ask people to tell you about what's in your pipeline. Try not to burn the time of others with scenarios that don't have a broad appeal to the team.

This is based on the concept of something referred to as "deliberate skill practice." I first heard that concept used in a book called *Talent is Overrated*, in which Geoffrey Colvin did a study of high performers and asked a simple and commonly asked question: are great performers just born to be great performers, or can great performers be taught to be great performers? The answer was consistent, across industry, arts, sports—great performers become great performers because they more consistently participate in something referred to as deliberate skill practice, where the people who care about being top performers seek out drills, exercises, and experts in the field to help them constantly grow and improve their game, whether the game is sales, chess, or football.

Topics could include any of the following:

- Your best intro to somebody you never met
- How do we build meaningful strategic partners
- Going from new account to best account
- Best voicemails to get a return call
- We charge more than they do; now what?

Keep working on a custom list of drills and exercises that relate to your group. Don't wait for an annual sales meeting to do some practice. That would be like LeBron showing up for the start of the season and saying, "Willing to give you guys two days of practice, and then I got this from there, see you at the games."

That doesn't happen.

This leads me to another concept that could happen at the sales practice or outside of the practice.

SYSTEM #5: SCRIMMAGE/DRESS REHEARSAL

I used to call this role play, but when you put down role play as the topic for the weekly practice, everybody ends up with big meetings scheduled with customers that could only meet at that time.

I prefer scrimmage/dress rehearsal/walk-through—maybe this happens in the weekly practice, and it definitely occurs outside of the practice.

I don't mean just talking about what's going to happen with that sales call; I mean actually acting out the entire call from "good to meet you" to "looking forward to working with you."

One person plays the role of the salesperson, another is the primary buyer, CEO, etc., and somebody else plays another role at the client company (CFO, IT director, etc.)

Everybody has done this at some point in their career; most people I meet don't like it, and because we don't like it, we don't do it.

Liking it has nothing to do with the point. Just like a marathon runner has a day to train for hills in the heat of the day to work on their endurance, but may not like hills. Like I have now said many times, you have to fall in love with the process. It's the process you can count on. Each individual sales call is going to have a lot of variables beyond your control. Your ability to adeptly get to the things that matter most is what will tend to separate you from the rest of the pack.

A client I have worked with for years has made a dedicated effort to constantly work on their game. A few years back, one of their people based in Atlanta saw an RFP go out from an international name company looking for new vendors.

Normally not very exciting, as these can often turn out to be giant wastes of time—perhaps the purchasing department looking to earn their keep and lean on their current vendor for some type of concessions. The lead sales guy, named Chris, reached out to me, and we talked through some ideas on how to get noticed.

We made it on the approved vendor list, which he felt was a win for future business potential. We gathered with some other key people being brought into the account and ran a key strategy session and scrimmage for how we could get taken seriously, and eventually made it to the top five. At this point, we ran several additional scrimmages, working through exactly how we would get from the purchasing department over to the business side of the account, and eventually, it came down to us versus the incumbent. The incumbent, by the way, was about the best competitor we had ever run into. Smart, great reputation, excellent quality of work—they had had the account for several years, and it was a $13 million per year piece of business.

We took that account from them. I can tell you why, too. You guessed it. We outworked them prior to ever meeting with them. I am certain that the incumbent took it for granted that they would renew the business per usual and didn't put the cycles into it that we did.

We timed exactly when the president of our company would contact the CMO of the client company. We worked through exactly how we could build enough consensus among their team to be willing to break free from their current vendor.

Often, the game is won before it starts, based on the level of preparation going into the game. If you think that just showing up for your calls is enough to consistently win at the highest level, you are probably missing out.

If you are not winning at least 40 to 80 percent of the deals that you compete for, then there is a problem, and you need to fix it. Again, the disciplined investment on the front end, clearing time in people's calendars, so that the people in your company can do the hard work of developing skills, is what will lead to that increased conversion rate. Once you get to above 80 percent, then perhaps you are not charging enough?

I have yet to meet any company that didn't have another ten percentage points to gain in conversion rate, and when you look at your overall cost of sales (see our cost of sales calculator on ChrisJenningsGroup.com) and look at what it really costs you to go to market over and over again and not win, it might just inspire you to put in the prep time.

I know we get busy; I know we all run fast. I promise you that developing these focused disciplines will pay back dividends over and over. Sales is not just a numbers game. It is a chess game that can be improved upon in every facet. Getting 1 percent better every day leads to some incredible performance and payoffs.

Going through a career, making $100K per year, closing 30 percent of your deals is not nearly as fun as making $300K per year and converting 60 percent of your deals. Add that up over a thirty-year career, and that puts an extra $6 million in your pocket. That's a good problem to have.

Leaders, I implore you to diligently build space in your teams' calendars to adopt these practices.

Individual performers who work for companies that don't do this, start doing it on your own. With us, with your peers, and with other colleagues.

Once you start doing the scrimmages regularly—**get out the video.**

Every time you run one of these scrimmages, the important thing is to start to capture live examples that can be shared later with the team. You want to try to capture a highlight reel of all the nuanced situations that your team would encounter for calling on both brand new prospects and existing clients.

My basic belief is most salespeople have never seen what a world-class sales call looks like. If you have never seen one, how would you possibly know how to run one?

No doubt we have all seen examples of poorly run calls. I don't play football, but I have seen it on TV. If I were to play catch with a football, I have an idea of how it's supposed to be thrown.

Where do you go to get great examples of what a world-class sales call looks like? That has been in short supply for a long time.

Once again, "Monkey see, monkey do; you just need to pick the right monkey."

Odds are you have had examples that were OK, but not world-class. Ideally, with the guidance from this book, you start to build your own library with all the examples you or your team would want.

It's how people like to learn these days. They watch a video. YouTube has some content; if you can find world-class level, please let me know. In the meantime, go to our website ChrisJenningsGroup.com, download whatever appeals to you, and then use that as a platform to start building your own content.

If you start doing the things I have shared, that will get you a long way toward your goals. Let's keep building.

SYSTEM # 6: WORLD-CLASS ONBOARDING PROGRAM

One of the best things you can do to set the tone with both new hires and new customers is to develop outstanding onboarding programs for both.

This sets the tone for the kind of relationship you want to have with your new people.

My favorite example of how to **onboard** new people is the Navy SEALs. I had the good fortune to sit in on a program delivered by a captain of the SEALs in San Diego. At the time, he had been running their onboarding and training program for the last couple of decades, and he shared some of their standards regarding the way they bring people in and up.

First, it's extremely difficult to get accepted into the program. Secondly, it's a two-and-a-half-year journey to complete the program before you are assigned to a SEAL team. Only 13 percent of the people who enter the program actually graduate and get assigned to a SEAL team. But if you do get assigned to a SEAL team, and you're asked to carry out a mission, what happens?

Answer: you carry out the mission! They never come back and say, "Well, we would really like to carry out the mission, but the boats we have are kind of small and crowded, and last time I ended up with a bit of a back thing, so maybe we could invest in some bigger boats, and then we will go out and run some more missions."

If you or your team has a propensity for excuse-making, this has to stop. We hit this earlier. All the nonsense about *if we had more special pricing for new customers, maybe we could waive the setup charges, maybe somebody could set up my appointments for me, my last company had a really good lead generation program.* All excuses, which maybe we bought into, and maybe not. Excuse-making is a slippery slope. The main point here is to look at the focus of control. If it's in your control, double down, do more of it, and/or do it better than you used to.

If it's out of your control, don't let it slow you down.

A Green Beret named Chris Miller shared a story about leading a team dropped into Iraq to secure the oil platforms during the Iraq War. He was told to expect heavy casualties. His mind at the time could have gone to *we are just going to have to accept losses* (of his teammates' lives, by the way, not just an "off" sales month). He planned out the mission, and he and his entire team all survived. We know it can be done, but you must prepare your team.

On the other side of the excuse coin, sometimes I hear sales leaders blame their people for lack of results: *this person is just lazy, they don't prospect enough, they want to give away the store.*

It really is a mutual responsibility to prepare our teams for the competitive situations we all face and give the team the best chance for success.

Ideally, if you are doing all the things I suggest in this book, if you hire somebody today, two weeks prior to their start date, you can give them a login and a passcode to a web address where they can listen to what a world-class sales call sounds like—your industry, your company. They can watch recorded video of what a world-class sales call looks like—your industry, your company. That new hire shows up to work on day one with a pretty good idea of what the target looks like. If you don't do that, there is a real good chance that the new hire wanders around your company for the first six to twelve months comparing your organization to other organizations and letting you know what the old company used to do, as an early foundational moment for an excuse when the numbers aren't achieved down the road.

If this is set up correctly, and by the way, I am not talking about a huge investment in money here, your new hire knows immediately that they joined an extremely professional organization, and they realize they will need to step up their game and bring it every day.

We all have a high gear, a low gear, and a medium gear. To a degree, it's human nature to do the minimum. There are a lot of biological and evolutionary drivers sending impulses internally to do the minimum and conserve energy; it's a survival instinct.

Reminder, this is not an overnight process to install. It will evolve over many months and years. But once the process is set in place, you use less energy because the process is already there. The improvements on the process only enhance the results, and so on. Most small to medium size companies I see lose the intention behind the process and get swallowed up by the "Urgent/Important" or "Not important." Thank you, Stephen Covey for that. If you haven't read Covey's book, *The 7 Habits of Highly Effective People*, it's costing you money. Just saying.

Make a start. Get the content created. Contact us if you want some starter packages to help make it easier on you or just DIY. In either case, make the investment in your people and watch how big the returns are.

In my opinion, the best investments you can make are in people.

My return out of the stock market is a very boring 6 percent per year over the course of my investing lifetime.

I have seen investments in people warrant 20 to 100 percent per year, and there really is no limit.

As a leader of your organization, you just need to make the decision that investing in your people is a priority.

If you are an individual contributor, and you don't currently work for a company that has this philosophy, then no excuses. Invest in yourself. Find a performance coach. Come to us or seek one out elsewhere. I can promise you the money will pay back handsomely.

My college tuition at UCLA was $759 per year when I started there. After increases, it was a four-plus-year investment of roughly $5K (crazy how cheap in-state fees were back then).

Post college. No MBA, or other graduate degree, I would estimate my personal out-of-pocket investment in myself in various coaching programs and additional learnings to be about $300K. The return on my college degree when I was seventeen to twenty-one years old with an underdeveloped frontal cortex, not huge.

The return on my post-college personal investment has to be well over 1,000 percent, no typo, well over 1,000 percent—get busy, keep learning, and become a student of the game.

SYSTEM # 7: FIELD RIDES

This has always been a favorite thing of mine to do. We do them as a normal course during a new assignment with a new client to get to know the ins and outs of each business we work with. I love third-party objective feedback. Memory is completely subjective. We all color in our memory to fit our own story, so the only real way to get awareness of what is actually happening around us is to get some third-party perspective on how we are interacting with those around us.

There are two kinds of **field rides** that I like to recommend going on. (This applies whether you are a salesperson or a sales leader.)

The Power Ride

On the **Power Ride**, the leader is involved. They are there to get some doors opened that might stay closed without their presence; they are there to get decisions made that might linger without their involvement.

If you are the CEO, I would recommend, at a minimum, you get out once a year to your top twelve customers and see them face-to-face. Ideally, I would suggest seeing your top twenty-four customers twice per year. If you are there that often, you have established deeper connections to your client company, and it becomes very unlikely for you to lose the business or have the account underperform versus its potential.

On the **Power Ride**, you are also there to demonstrate what should be happening on the average world-class sales call. Your people need to see that call played out. The selection should be made in advance to determine the twelve biggest upside potential accounts that the individual salesperson has in their territory, and bringing along the extra muscle could really move the needle in a measurable way.

The Observation Ride

The second type of **field ride** is just like you would imagine: pure observation. Its only purpose is for you as the leader to observe how the individual salesperson handles themselves on a call.

So, as the leader, you will need to set it up.

Don't say this:

"Danny here has been telling me great things about your potential, and I wanted to come along and see what we could do to increase the amount of business we are doing." No, no, and more no.

Say this instead:

"Hi Jan. So glad we are getting a chance to meet. I have been super interested in learning more about you and your company. Danny here is the person most familiar with your business, and he is going to be your go-to person going forward, so I want to turn this meeting back over to him."

Let the person you are riding with run the call. It's an **Observation Ride, so be quiet.**

Whoever is running the call has the ball. The call should be moving along in a decent manner, and at some point, the ball may pop out of the salesperson's hands, bounce around the ground, and land right in front of your feet. What do you want to do? Pick it up. Score some points. Do a victory dance in the endzone. I am going to explicitly ask you not to do that.

Here's the problem. When you pick up the ball, what's the messaging to the salesperson?

Yup, "I don't believe in you. Only I can fix problems of this magnitude; you really don't have to work that hard. You should call me to fix all your problems." Basically, the exact opposite of what we should want the learnings to be.

Now for you sales leaders who are also looked at as the best salesperson, it's going to be especially hard for you to let go of this. This is no place to feed your ego. You are trying to build up your team's confidence, not tear it down.

For you CEOs who have set up the sales department in this fashion, this is your problem. If you only have one excellent seller in the whole company, and they are also your sales leader, they hold a lot of power, and it can get used against the best interests of the team and the organization.

Sales leaders, you can't be great at everything. There are so few examples of great player-coaches. The only one I am even aware of was Bill Russell with the Boston Celtics for a very short period.

Most of the time, great coaches were good role players, but not superstar performers themselves.

The key here is that you have to be motivated, and probably incentivized, by the performance of the team more so than your own personal performance. More on this later.

Here's the other problem with stepping in on an observation call: think about the messaging to the customer.

"This salesperson isn't your go-to person; I am your go-to person." Now, what ends up happening is you have too many customers reaching out to you for things that your team should be completely capable of handling, further rendering you less effective as a sales leader and becoming more of an account manager. I have lots of ideas about how you can grow your people and the business with each customer, but unless you are specifically on a **Power Ride**, then you have to let your team run the call their way—even if you see opportunities to improve the call. Hard to do, yes, but if you are ever going to get out ahead of the problem, then you need to let your people run their calls as they normally do.

I remember going on a field ride with a salesperson (Nick) from a client company of ours, a very common part of our process early on in client engagements. Nick, by the way, is a very good salesperson and still works for the company today. If you met him, you would want to hire him.

I met Nick in the parking lot in El Cajon, California. Nick looked at me and asked, "Are you going to run the call today?" My response was, "Definitely not. This is all you. Chris Jennings, new with the company." This is about all that comes out of my mouth during the client meeting. We get back to the parking lot, and Nick looks at me again and says, "How did I do?" All normal stuff so far.

Formula for Feedback

Three Positive Observations. I always find three things that I liked about how the person I'm riding with ran the call. That day I said to Nick:

"Nick, your vibe and connection with the customer was excellent; you clearly know the industry well, and I believe the customer felt you were sincere in wanting to help him address his issues." (The company sold shipping and logistics-related services.)

I like passing out the sincere compliments before I highlight the areas for improvement. It's reassuring, and there is always something that they did well.

The max I ever offer for suggestions to improve is two. By the way, that day, Nick made about two dozen errors, which is average for us. Twenty-four times when the salesperson went left, but I would have gone right. Think about it: even the winning team in any sport usually has a couple dozen or more miscues they wish hadn't happened. This isn't a bad thing so much; this is just the reality of so many sales calls.

That day I said, "Nick, you know that intake form that you have to fill out to quote the job accurately? Well, you had it lying on the customer's desk the whole time. I could see the customer continue glancing at it, wondering what it was and when you were going to get to it. Then, when it came time to fill that thing out, it just got really clunky in there."

Nick says to me, "You know. I have always struggled with how to get the information that I need to quote the job accurately without feeling like I'm annoying the customer. It always feels awkward to me."

What did we do? We ran drills at the **Weekly Skill Practice** on how to get the information we needed to accurately quote the job without the customer feeling like we were burning up a lot of their time unnecessarily. This is a really common issue. The salesperson often apologetically tries to rush through getting the information they need, and the prospect senses their anxiety, picks up on it, and it can be a real disconnect for both parties, often leaving some important details completely out and/or inaccurate.

For the rest of the two dozen issues, I went back to the two partners who owned the company and worked through a prioritization list of which of those might have the most impact on the sales process and overall outcomes, and we created drills on each one of those. As I said, Nick is a great sales guy, so if Nick is having this issue, everybody is likely having this issue.

I think the key here, once again, is creating an atmosphere where we all want to get better all the time. That any sales call is a practice call, and each one of those gives us an opportunity to improve.

I have often suggested to sales folks who I work with that they go out on some "practice calls." You know, calls that maybe you don't really want to, or need to, win, or even really care what the outcomes are. What ends up happening on these calls, as a rule?

You are so relaxed and free-flowing in your conversation, so unattached to the outcome, that your prospect senses that they probably need your help more than you need them. Guess what happens? Yup, they want to buy from you!

Please remember, people love to buy things; they hate to be sold. Buying stuff has always been fun; being sold on something has always felt wrong.

Once you practice some of these tools in a practice call environment, you start to see the power in being truly unattached to the outcome. This is something I call **Abundance Mentality**.

Abundance Mentality is when you finally figure out that there are likely way more prospects out there than there are of you. The reality is the average prospect does need you more than you need them. You just need to stay steady, calm, and have a relaxed confidence.

Sooner or later, it dawns on you. That they are all practice calls. We aren't running out of prospects. You don't have to be perfect on every call. It's **just a conversation.**

Hopefully, you are starting to see how this all fits together.

- You go on the field rides and look for areas to work on.
- You develop specific deliberate skill practice sessions around each specific aspect of the ideal sales call model.
- You run scrimmages to demonstrate world-class performance.
- You capture this on video.
- You build out the video and call recordings to create your onboarding.
- You repeat the process again, and again, and again.

This is what world-class organizations do. This is all possible if you set your intention and just go to work on it. If you get confused or need help, just holler. Talk to us or somebody else who is in the habit of doing this all the time, so you can draft off their efforts and get this to work for you even faster, with less energy expended.

SYSTEM #8: THE MYSTERY SHOP

As I said earlier, I love third-party objective feedback. I wish we could all remember things accurately, but the reality is we are always modifying our memory to fit how we would like to remember things.

This falls under the "trust but verify" category.

People try harder when they know they are being watched. We all have multiple gears inside of us, and **Mystery Shopping** on a regular basis kicks the team into a higher gear. This is also sometimes called "secret shopper"; essentially, it's hiring someone to pose as a customer to see how we are handling our customers.

I like doing **Mystery Shops** for a couple of reasons, but number one: we all have a lot of great people doing a really good job, and I like to catch them doing a good job.

My youngest daughter, Mattie, had her first job working as a hostess at a Mimi's café. She had been working there maybe for a month, and she came home from work one day and said, "Dad, the mystery shopper called today. I got all the lunch specials exactly right!" She was beaming with pride. The manager had come over and said, "Good job, Mattie!" I also think she scored a box of bran muffins as a reward and recognition for her execution of the plays they had drawn up.

That **Mystery Shop** really was a confidence boost for her. She very quickly applied for the job as a server and was hired for that role. When a new flagship location opened, she walked in and got hired on the spot for that role, and that confidence has carried forward to this day.

You are also going to learn about other opportunities that probably would have stayed hidden if you weren't doing the **Mystery Shop**.

We were working with a construction-related company focused on the outside team, who was convinced you had to be "low bid" to win work. That is not necessarily true, so we were chipping away at that.

In the meantime, we decided to do a project with "The Counter People." They were a busy group of **Special Teams** players that fielded most of the incoming inquiries from customers or prospects looking for pricing and availability on such and such.

We did four **Mystery Shops**. Here's what we found:

- Three out of four times, they never asked for a phone number. They were more than content to shoot out a quote to a Gmail address.
- Zero out of four times did they ever ask any qualifying questions. Questions like, "Hey, who do you normally go to in situations like these? What kind of work do you focus on? How did you find your way to us?" None of these were ever asked.
- Zero out of four times (this is the worst offense, in my opinion) did they ever call the corresponding sales rep and say, "Hey, somebody new just called in from your territory; you should probably go check out that job site and see what they have going on there."

So let me ask you: who is responsible for those missed opportunities?

If you said leadership, you were right. Not sure if you have read the book *Extreme Ownership* written by a couple of Navy SEALs. The basic lesson of the book is this: everything that happens on your watch, with your team, under your command, is your responsibility.

In this case, it was a guy named Kevin. By the way, Kevin runs a fantastically profitable company. Last time I was in Kevin's office, I'm pretty sure he was on the phone with his wife, about to leave for Positano, which, if you haven't been there, is a pretty nice place in Italy.

I'm not worried about Kevin. Most people I meet who run companies have already figured out a good formula for success, and you are likely to stay on that course for the duration.

I am worried about his people. I know that team well. They are a bunch of nice, hard-working people who get up at 0 dark 30 and try to wander onto construction sites, hoping not to get thrown out and hoping to strike up a relationship with a new field superintendent, project manager, or other customer.

The counter people are also hard-working, moving from demand to demand, pulled in multiple directions, and really trying to do the best they can each day, as most of us are.

The reason to set up and adhere to these systems is to make people's jobs easier. For the team to get more done, requiring less energy, because they are functioning within a well thought out process that doesn't require them to over-exert constantly and have an energy reserve to apply toward their customers.

If you have all these implemented and everybody knows their role, the experience for the team member, the leader, and the customer are all improved. Tackling the one-off situations with more ease and confidence, constantly working toward a better and improved outcome.

That, in my opinion, is how it could and should be. This is why I am writing this right now, to hopefully pass on some of what I have seen and experienced so that others may have energy left to invest wherever else it is required and desired.

SYSTEM # 9: UNBIASED ASSESSMENT TOOLS—THE 4 SCIENCES

Before starting in the field I now work, on my way out of a role that felt very unsatisfying, I completed a personality profile to lead me to a more fulfilling career. Included as one of the suggestions was that I consider becoming a poultry scientist. I didn't know that was an option; I passed on that.

Another assessment tool that I used suggested that I have no business being in sales at all based on my acquired skills. My extraordinarily low income that year, chronicled much earlier in this book, might have seemed to justify that assertion, but I was passionate about what I started. I saw glimpses of where my future successes could lie, and I was relentlessly dedicated to the process.

So, the fact that I sit here today ready to suggest to you that there are assessment tools based in real behavioral science that are worth exploring may seem puzzling to you. I have worked hard to keep an open mind and become a lifelong learner, which to me, keeps life interesting, and hopefully slows down the aging process.

The reasons I rely on and use these specific tools are two-fold:

1. I have spoken in great detail about the trends and common observations I have made over decades in the field. However, individual coaching must be tailored to the individual. We are all created equal, but we are not all created the same. Knowing the tendencies in our personal profiles helps us create a path to improved performance and significantly improve our communication skills.
2. If I am trying to match somebody to a new role, having some third-party objective feedback that doesn't have anything to do with what schools we went to or what similar backgrounds we had, but is just purely a data-driven indication of what would come more easily to one person than another also just makes sense. Yes, I could be a good corporate citizen and follow protocols, but there was a lot in me from the beginning that could indicate to a prospective employer about how much work it

would take to get me productive, and if somebody wanted to hire me, giving them a what to do and what not to do scenario on me, would be an overwhelmingly positive thing to do for everybody involved.

After years of experimenting with different tools and behavioral sciences, here are the four methods I lean on to accomplish the aforementioned objectives.

First Behavioral Science: DISC

Odds are, at this point in your career, you have taken a **DISC** profile. Although, there are several **DISC** providers who repackage the advice in a myriad of ways. Not all are created equal.

DISC divides the world into quadrants, where each one of us has a primary behavioral style and secondary behavioral style. We tend to follow those styles in all areas of our lives, and those tendencies are not likely to vary unless, perhaps, we are under intense pressure. Even under pressure, many of us don't deviate from our natural style; the more we deviate from our natural **DISC** style in our communication, the more stress is created in our life. It takes a lot of thought and energy to have multiple modalities in our hip pocket for dealing with life on life's terms.

Below are the four DISC styles.

D—Drivers tend to be direct, willing to take risks, less concerned with feelings or detail, focused on a goal, and moving fast. **Animal reference—The Lion.**

I—Influencers tend to be moving fast, risk takers, big picture, talkative, and really enjoy the spotlight. **Animal reference—The Dolphin.**

S—Socializers tend to be friendly, empathetic, inclusive, risk-averse, slower, interested in people more than process. **Animal Reference—The Labrador.**

C—Analyticals tend to be scientific, careful and cautious, detailed and slower, exacting, and prioritizing process over people, very risk-averse. **Animal Reference—The Owl.**

None of these are right or wrong, just different ways of prioritizing how to communicate in the world. (Note, if you are high D, you probably think everybody who doesn't see the world like you do is wrong.)

Understanding DISC and how to alter your approach from what feels most natural to you to what is the best way for your audience will help professionally in two ways. (This will help anyone at home too.)

1. Your team: why does Johnny feel the need to go over so much detail? Their **DISC** profile can probably answer that for you. We recommend having your **DISC** profile in your email signature or outside your office to give the world a fighting chance to tailor their message to you in the best way possible.
2. Your customers: wouldn't it be easier, and I love things to be easier, if instead of being a one-size-fits-all robot, you found a way to tailor your presentation and entire customer experience to the way your customer communicates?

All that for the first science.

Second Behavioral Science: Motivators and Driving Forces

We all have motivational tendencies that guide us. Certainly, it would be good to know if you are more motivated by being in charge and getting it done on your own or by collaborating with a big group.

Or understanding do you want to make judgments based on your instincts or by doing more research?

There are twelve Motivational Profiles:

- Resourceful vs. Selfless
- Objective vs. Harmonious
- Collaborative vs. Commanding
- Intentional vs. Altruistic
- Receptive vs. Structured
- Intellectual vs. Instinctive

Once we know our profiles for our teams, we can use or avoid specific language just based on this. We can help people pick the right roles for themselves rather than put them in situations that might work against them. Ultimately, I think we are all happiest when we are surrounded by a supportive culture that has similar values and clearly understands the reasons for somebody having different priorities.

Take a guess where you fit, and perhaps re-look at it after you complete the assessments.

Third Behavioral Science: Learned Skills and Competencies

We have identified twenty-five basic skills that will help people make great salespeople, leaders, and a multitude of other roles in the world.

For the purposes of this read, I am referencing how to use these tools for customer-facing roles, but I have helped organizations hire CEOs, investment personnel, project managers, and many other roles. The best executive recruiters use these tools to help them make the right choice, put the right person in the right role, and help new hires get up to speed more quickly than anyone would without the feedback in the assessment.

Fourth Behavioral Science: EQ (Emotional Intelligence)

I could have made the whole book about the EQ.

It's a really smart way to look at our ability to read and regulate emotion. Understanding our emotional state, being able to read the emotional state of the room, and then adjusting ours to meet that of our audience are absolute musts.

EQ measures that as well as our motivational state. Life in sales is filled with highs and lows and a preponderance of things "not going our way."

If you are engaged in the process of what you do, are not overly attached to the outcome, and are convinced you have something super useful to offer, your motivation should come from that source and not be overly dependent on the results.

We need to continue to learn from our "losses," and turn losses into lessons that make us better equipped to help the next individual we encounter.

Several books are written on emotional intelligence, and we have built multiple coaching sessions that you can download or participate in to learn more about this topic—all available at ChrisJenningsGroup.com.

All too often, many in sales feel the need to create a wall around themselves, so they don't feel the hurt of things not going their way. The downside is you are then walled off from multiple emotional cues and clues that are needed to understand and could be put to good use.

You want your prospect or customer to feel that you truly "get them."

There cannot be any disconnects, or that customer will disconnect from you. I encourage you to lean into what motivates you. Become a real detective in pursuit of what makes you tick and learn to study people to better understand what makes them do what they do. This will prepare you to make incredible connections with your customers and all those who you encounter.

This will enable you to spread the good word about what you offer and to cast a wider net of deep, meaningful connections.

SYSTEM #10: HIRING AND RECRUITING

As I write this, we are still feeling and dealing with the effects of the pandemic. Everywhere I go, people tell me they are having a hard time hiring good people. As a reminder to all leaders, there are millions of good people out there; the search for finding and keeping the best talent is meant to be a never-ending one that must be a focus of ours if we are to really identify the best talent and be prepared to weave them into our companies when ready.

So here is what I suggest: recruit like collegiate coaches recruit for their athletes. Here's how it works:

First, they start really early. Coach K, Coach Cronin, Coach Saban—guaranteed all these coaches have identified this year's team multiple years before they start the season.

All of them have great relationships with high school coaches and club coaches around the country and around the world that have loyalties to them, their team, and their staff of coaches.

For example, a fourteen-year-old future phenom is in a club program in Minnesota, and it's the middle of summer, and that coach calls up Coach K and says, "Hey Coach K, I know it's the middle of summer, and you are probably trying to get some downtime before the season starts, but I got a kid in my program, and I really want you to see him first. I know he's only fourteen years old, but you really need to see this kid in action."

When Coach K and his coaching staff get on a plane and fly up to Minnesota to watch the kid play in a tournament, it's a really big deal. The whole team knows they are there. That kid's family knows they are there. The entire balance of that fourteen-year-old's high school career he is hoping that Coach K offers him that scholarship to Duke (fill in school of your choice), and that he/she gets that opportunity.

That's how I suggest you recruit.

So here is what you do specifically:

Go to your customers, your vendors, your employees, and other

strategic partners in the marketplace you serve, and let them know what you want. Say something like this:

"We are always on the hunt for great people. If you ever have someone you meet that you think is a great individual, and they are just working for the wrong company, it would mean the world to me if you could connect us. Are you open to that?"

Sometimes you incentivize them financially, sometimes not. The key here is to be **constantly recruiting**.

When you meet that great potential hire, they are most likely already employed. Great people have jobs, and lots of people want to hire them. You have to show them you are different based on your actions.

> **Don't say this:**
>
> "What do I have to do to get you to come work for me? What's it going to cost me?" It's too abrupt, it's likely too much change, and you are not taking into account several factors that might be in play here.
>
> **Say this instead:**
>
> "Anthony, you seem like a really talented individual. Someday, it would be cool if we got a chance to work together. I know you have a job, and I'm not trying to get in the way of what you have going on, but someday, if your situation ever changes, it would be great to have you and me on the same team; I hope you would keep that in mind?"

Pay that person an honest and sincere compliment. Think for a second. How often does that happen to people, where somebody stops them and pays them such a highly complimentary tribute? Instantly, they feel better about themselves. Instantly, you become a special person in their life. They go home and tell their spouse, friend, or significant other, "Hey, I had somebody try to hire me today. I told them no for now, but it got me thinking."

How often does their current boss stop them and say, "Anthony, you are a super talented person; it is great having you as a team member." No, they say, "Hey, when am I going to see the report you promised me?"

If you are on your game, you put that new potential hire on your...

TOP 10 RECRUITING LIST

Every four to six months, you reach out to them. Let them know you are still here. Take an active interest in their lives.

> **Don't say this:**
>
> "So you ready to come work for me yet? I had somebody quit recently, and I am desperate to find a replacement." Once again, this exhibits a real lack of emotional intelligence, and you are likely to scare away as many as, or more than, you attract with that.
>
> **Say this instead:**
>
> "Hey Anthony, how's it going? I saw your Yankees were way off base this year, and I needed to ask you what was going on with the team. Am I going to see you at the conference in May? Let's for sure grab dinner or a drink."

It's OK to repeat what you said to them initially; I just want you to be sensitive to where they are at. If that individual is having the best year of their career financially, this may not be the time; however, if he/she is traveling way more than they like, missing their family, and you offer something that may be better...

Maintain interest, but you have to be looking out for what's best for them. Don't rush this; I promise when the timing is right, they will call you. If you consistently work through your list of future hires and have great conversations with them along the way, I promise that half of those people will end up working for you.

It might take an average of two to five years per hire, but you probably will have to wait until the circumstances are **right for them.**

The smart and most successful sales leaders we coach are committed to doing this one to five hours per week, every week. In fact, the top sales leaders in the world all have a bench of people following them. Once they go somewhere, their phones ring off the hook. "Hey Leia, I noticed you changed companies; what brought you over there?" "Hey, can you get me in? I'm ready for a change, and I would really enjoy working for you."

Top sales leaders have been doing this for years. If you are in a leadership role and you are not doing this, get busy.

I work with a tremendous team of partners who run most of our assignments. Once I was speaking at a business event for CEOs, and one of the people in attendance saw our team roster, and they proceeded to tell me this story:

"I know Anthony. Anthony is a great guy." This is true. Anthony

Mayo is a very talented coach, speaker, salesperson, and sales leader.

He continued, "Anthony used to call on me years ago when he was a sales rep for XYZ company. The company he worked for was horrible. I bought from Anthony twice, and both times the product that I bought failed. I told Anthony, 'I love you, man, but you are out of here.'"

Imagine a talented salesperson like an Anthony Mayo, who goes out, finds a new customer, and gets them to buy from them, and both times their company lets the customer down. If you were Anthony in that circumstance, what would you want to do?

If you already have them on your **Top 10 Recruiting List**, you are probably their next phone call. It usually sounds like this. "Hey Chris, what do you say we go to lunch?" This is usually code for, "I'm ready to come work for you now." This is how you recruit.

Stay way ahead of it, have a bench, share with your team that you have a bench, and always make room for a superstar.

I have heard a statistic that 3 percent of the world's salespeople sell 65 percent of the world's goods and services. Crazy but, I think, fairly accurate. About 17 percent of the salespeople in the world account for the next 17 percent, and the remaining 80 percent of the world fights over the scraps and the remaining 20 percent.

Now, if you are a salesperson, let that set your mind to what is possible. So what if your quota is $1 million per year? Start thinking today, how do I make my territory a $10 million or $20 million territory?

If you are in leadership, and you find someone currently available who has the potential to sell $10 million a year when your average team member is at $2 million per year, get them a job on your team. Don't wait; somebody else will grab them in a second.

Stop depending on the job boards as your primary recruiting source. I don't think Coach K ever had an ad on Craigslist: "Looking for graduating seniors, with good athletic ability, willing to show up to practice on time."

If the job boards are really your best source, then you are settling; you are not doing the work to go find people. Hiring recruiters works sometimes, but they need to be a great recruiter, and you will need to pay them top dollar.

Don't negotiate with recruiters. Let's say that their average fee is $35K per hire, and you think you are a great negotiator, and they agree to send you people at $10K per hire. You are going to pay lots of money for resumes. Those people won't have any better track record for success than anybody else.

One more story about recruiting that was told to me by a client in Birmingham, Alabama.

He was on a golf course at his country club when an announcement came out over the loudspeaker.

"We are closing the course due to the fact that we have a very special guest coming today, and we are requesting that all members immediately report to the clubhouse." Clearly, this was an odd occurrence, and my client was quite intrigued as to who it might be.

When he got to the clubhouse, he learned that the newly hired football coach for the University of Alabama, Nick Saban, was in the clubhouse and had offered to address the community. Among many other updates, he shared this one excerpt from his talk.

Nick Saban told the crowd that day, "No disrespect to the former coach, but when we got here, they had about fifty-eight recruits on the recruiting board; today, we have over seven hundred. I can promise you, our team is about to get a whole lot better."

Stop looking for shortcuts. Stop making excuses and find ways to implement this system and all the other systems I have been sharing with you. Armed with these, over time, you will build an incredible team. Over time, you will attract great talent because great players want to play on great teams.

Help your team and your company develop the reputation in the industry that you are different. Other people will judge you based on your actions. People often judge themselves on their intentions. If you are a sales leader who has the intention of installing the systems I have described here, but you aren't actually doing it, then get some help.

Find somebody to do it for you. But not doing it is resigning yourself to mediocrity, being average. I know that in a great market, being average might seem good enough, but if you want to outperform the market, you must outwork the market. Install these systems, and you will be joining an elite few.

IN SUMMARY

Chart your progress every ninety days by using the **10 Systems**

Score Sheet, available on our website. Even when we are hired to implement these systems, we try to grow by about five to ten points per quarter.

If you do that consistently over a one- to two-year period, and you started the first year at a thirty-eight, and you got to sixty-eight by the end of year one, and you got to eighty-eight by the end of year two, I can virtually assure you that you are now printing money. I have never seen a company that got their top **10 Sales Systems** scores **above seventy** that wasn't one of the most profitable, most highly sought-after companies in their space.

The team members will be loyal to the company that helped them develop these skills. More will get accomplished with less energy expended. The word will get out that this is a great place to work, and others will want to join your team. Sounds pretty good, yes? Work toward it, and it will happen.

Here is a recap of the **10 Sales Systems** provided below:

CHRIS JENNINGS GROUP

SALES, LEADERSHIP, & CLIENT RETENTION

10 Systems to Build a Championship Team   Scale 1-10

1. Go Live 4 Hours Per Day   _____

2. Special Teams   _____

3. Call Recording System   _____

4. Weekly Deliberate Skill Practice   _____

5. Video Scrimmage   _____

6. Onboarding New People/Special Teams   _____

7. Field Rides-Power-Observation   _____

8. Mystery Shopping   _____

9. Individual/Team Assessment Tools   _____

10. Hiring & Recruiting Systems   _____

                                        Your Score: _____

                                        Today's Date: _____

                                        Your Goal:

PART 5

THE SALES LEADERS TOOL KIT

———

So far, everything that I have covered ends up in your playbook. Some additional key areas you will want to add to your playbook include:

- CRM
- Pipeline management
- How to run one-to-ones
- Compensation planning
- Sales team structure

The playbook has value for the team and its individual players when the concepts are implemented, refined, and then taught to others.

When we learn new information, there is a simple formula for developing new skills:

1. Tell your audience what you want them to learn.

2. Demonstrate what you want them to learn.
3. Have them tell you what you told them.
4. Have them demonstrate what they just learned.

So, for all of you leaders, salespeople, and other professionals out there, you have to give away this information to keep it. Share the concepts with others so that they may follow your lead and so that you might better understand and internalize these concepts to ultimately become your concepts. If you want to tell people where you got this from, then great, we are happy to help.

If you want to just start sharing the information, there are so few original ideas left on this planet. If you want some tools and resources to help with implementation, we have included several great tools in a downloadable format on our website ChrisJenningsGroup.com.

I am sharing everything I have soaked up over forty-seven years (from twelve to fifty-nine) of door knocking, leading teams, and trying to help and inspire others to greater futures than they would have had without my influence.

I want you to do the same.

Let's tackle some of the remaining items to complete your playbook.

CRM DOS AND DON'TS

Don't do this:

1. Don't buy a CRM without a plan of how to use it and how it fits into your **30 Minute Success Plan**.
2. Don't expect the CRM to increase visibility of **Go Live** time if

you are not tracking the specific **Go Live** activities from those **30 Minute Success Plans.**

3. Don't start asking the team to track a bunch of new stuff in the CRM **that isn't equally as good for the individual producer as it is for the company.** I have seen several organizations that undervalue or resent the free time afforded a salesperson, and therefore, they start piling on tasks that really aren't sales related. If the activity isn't leading to more **Go Live** time, more opportunities, and an increase in total business with an existing client (see our next book, *Conversations Made Easy: The Client Retention Matrix*, a how-to guide to keeping clients around longer, with higher margins, and getting them to refer you to two clients per year), then don't ask them to track it. Only salesleading indicators go into the CRM. If the team is already averaging four hours per day of **Go Live** time, then get them admin help.

4. Don't neglect to get your sales team help once they've hit a certain production level in either gross margin and/or **Go Live** hours. If you can free them up to make more calls, ask for more referrals, and go on more appointments, then do it. Invest in admin and true back-office support, but don't make it too easy. Ideally, it is earned. This chicken or egg question is easy for me to solve. Take as much unnecessary administrative stuff away, hold people accountable for the activity, and if somebody drops below a certain production level, they lose support. This includes CRM entry. I have no problem if you pay someone else to do it, but only after proving a commitment to the activity for at least a 90- to 180-day period.

5. Don't let your team members spend more than thirty minutes a day entering info into a database. That would indicate something is really wrong, and it need to get fixed. Get an independent analysis of your current CRM to see where it is bogging down.

6. Don't throw away your old CRM just because you heard there is

a better one out there. There probably is, but that alone should not be the reason you chuck what you currently have. Most every CRM we have looked at has a pathway to success, and if it already talks to your ERP system, etc., you may be able to salvage it. There are so many great programs today.

Do this instead with your CRM:

1. Make sure every customer-facing **Special Teams player**, salesperson, CSR, etc., has at least three to five KPIs that are trackable in the CRM.
2. Build a dashboard so that you can see adherence to the KPI standards is met both daily and weekly. At a glance, you'll know your company is doing the things it is supposed to do.
3. Hang in there through the learning curve—inside of thirty to ninety days, you should be able to implement most of the functionality of the CRM throughout your sales team; if not, something is wrong. There may be other functions that still aren't aligned. Get with your CRM implementer, or call us for a recommendation.
4. Track conversion rates from both first contact, first appointment, and from proposal. All three measurements will provide excellent baselines and learnings for the whole company. Keep this on a trailing twenty-four-month basis and set alarms for trends up or down.
5. Make the statistics public to anybody inside the company. Company-wide access to help people be held accountable by all works great. This isn't public shaming. This is transparency, so if you have a top salesperson making $500K per year and an ops manager making $150K per year who wonders why, let them see for themselves what is being done to earn that level of income. This is a great comradery and collaboration tool. I am

not saying make everybody's comp structure public, just the activity and the results.

6. Be clear about what it takes to stay with the company and that lack of activity combined with lack of results would compromise their spot on the team. It's simple—if you are not achieving or exceeding your sales numbers on a regular basis, we need to be all over your activity. If you are blowing your numbers out of the water by a factor of 5x to the next person, it probably doesn't matter how many phone calls you made yesterday, but it does matter what else you are doing that is trackable that can be a shared learning for the team and the company.

7. Track pipeline by individual and by teams using something close to the following formula:

   A. **Name of the prospect.** Yes, publicly name all your prospects. You never know when somebody who works at your company is married to your prospect's CEO, CFO, etc. I am never worried about this leaking to competitors because we should win on our merits and the strength of our team.

   B. **On a scale of one to ten, the likelihood that this will close.** One meaning never; ten meaning a deal was signed, they paid, and they've already written you a reference to post on your website. By the way, I only want to track deals that are at least 50-50 or better; typically, a 25 percent chance of closing really means no chance of closing. I do allow some cheap fives now and then.

   C. **Born-on date.** This means: when did we first start talking? Most deals have momentum, a cadence, and a clear path to the finish line. Good deals are just good deals from the start. Bad deals, with low probability and very little executive sponsorship, are probably turned over to somebody new to learn from.

   D. **Next-step date.** This is the date and time of the next scheduled **Go Live** interaction. If there isn't a scheduled next step date and time, deduct twenty-five points from the probability. To be clear, this isn't, *I will call them on the first to see how it looks,* or, *they promised me feedback by the thirtieth*—if I see a bunch of dates on the first, the fifteenth, or the thirtieth, I pretty much know these aren't real.

E. **Other.** You can add anything you like here, such as size of deal, type of business, new products or services, and top three reasons they need you more than you need them—as long as you have the required four categories.

I know I started talking about this in the CRM section, but true confessions—if you didn't have a CRM, you could make everything I am talking about in these two hundred or so pages work extremely well. In fact, even with a CRM, I would suggest you put all this on your **Crack Board**—an actual dry-erase board hung on public display, which is called a Crack Board to remind you about the deals that you might forget about because they "fell through the cracks." Even if we haven't met, I am fairly certain you have forgotten to call back somebody you promised to call back, and a potentially good opportunity went bye-bye because, well, you let it fall through the cracks. The prospect didn't feel important enough to you, and there wasn't a scheduled next step; you get the picture.

I probably prefer the title of "**Top 10/Top 20 Board.**"

*New Opportunities

Name	1-10	Born on Date	NXT Step Date	Description	Initials
1 Hornblower	9	12/2	2/17	Hlc Panels wall laminates	LF/Jim
2 IB Roofing	8	10/11	1/30 (quote Accum)	Roofing	LF/Andy
3 Bergmann Group	8	1/19	Sending Samples 2/11	Medical Carts	LF
4 Carstens	9	2/2	3/2 (visit)	Medical Carts	Andy/Linda
5 Anthony Int'l	9	10/11	1/17 Conf Additional	Strips	JB/Andy
6 Harlott	9	6/2010	On-going	medical Carts	JB/Jim
7 Decture Surfaces	7	2/13	Took samples to put into market	Furniture	JB/Robin
8 Western Star	8	10/11/11	Andy visit 2/1w Portland	Rosewood-parts Door-ABS	LF
9 Innovative Solutions	5	1/12	Looking on samples from Brian	Veneer Cherry	LF
10 Fabcon	7	8/11	Follow up 2-29-12 market test	POP/ Fabricator	LF
11 Ryerson-Winnipeg	7	8/11	Color match on Vinyl	AVDEC /FABRICS	LF
12 Forbes Ind.	5	1/19	Robin follow up on quote	Hospitality Carts	LF/Jim/Andy
13 Navistar / StoreRidge	6	2005	Dropping Portable Visit	Dash Panels -Trucking	JB/Robin
14 Sika Sarnafil	8	1/24	3/22-3/23 →meet in orlando	Roofing ; Flashing	AP/Linda
					AP

The theory is this: You should have at least ten deals with a probability of seven or above at all times. If you look at your board and you only have two deals up there, what does that tell you? Yes! Get busy! **Go Live!** Fall in love with your process again.

On the high end, you should have no more than twenty deals with a seven or above at any one time. Why is that?

For sure, if you have thirty-five deals that are all seven, eight, or nine, the odds are you are not accurately qualifying any of these. They are clogging up your pipeline, and you may be overlooking the best deals in your pipeline and believing everything that ever gets said to you from a prospect, like most overly optimistic "that's how I got into sales in the first place" kind of people.

Stick to this system. If you get to twenty deals, and you want to add somebody else, somebody has to come off the board. **There are three ways off the board:**

1. They buy, you sign a contract, and off we go to the onboarding stages (see **BeUseful…Now**, or go to The Client Retention Matrix).
2. They come off as, "No thanks, we went in a different direction."
3. Solid Next Step, and you rebook a firm final next step date with an agreement that by the end of that meeting they either say, "Get out of my life forever. I can't believe anybody even works with you," or, "Here is your signed contract, let's get rolling."

The idea is this board is fluid, deals come on, and stay on the board for as little time as possible until they either move to the **Onboarding Board** (see my next book) or recycle into your prospecting systems.

Don't get too attached to opportunities, stay open to the next deal, and trust in your process, have faith in your process, be encouraged by your process.

RUNNING ONE-TO-ONES WITH YOUR DIRECT REPORTS

I have a simple formula for your weekly one-to-ones with each direct report.

Dedicate thirty to forty-five minutes per week to each direct report so they can have some time to connect with you on the areas most critical to them, and have a rotational focus on each meeting based on the needs or tenure of the person you are working with.

I always like to allow up to ten minutes for them to share successes and/or vent regarding stuff that was on their mind. Stay on point here, manage the clock, and move on to the focus for that week.

For example:

- **Week 1: Activity.** How are they performing versus their planned number of calls, appointments, referrals, etc.?
- **Week 2: Pipeline.** Look at their Top 10/20 Board and help them evaluate the quality of what is in the pipeline versus your expectation for both the quantity and quality of what they have identified.
- **Week 3: Recorded Calls.** Have them prepare by sending you one to three good calls or common challenges they are running into, so that you can listen to those calls in advance and be prepared to offer feedback.
- **Week 4: Field Ride Reviews.** Take some of the one-on-ones to work on the ongoing themes, both good and bad, that you keep seeing in their calls.

If you stick to something close to this rotation, it will keep you both accountable for their progress, and the structure of the one-to-ones will give them a greater connection to you and allow them to see a clear pathway forward.

SALES COMPENSATION DOS AND DON'TS

Don't do this:

1. Don't limit the upside that anybody can make. If you own or run a company, and you can build a comp structure that allows people unlimited success and opportunity via a robust comp plan, putting a cap on it will for sure send the best performers elsewhere. Don't worry if they make more money than you. Who cares! We should all wish for a team of high performers that makes lots of money and loves and appreciates us and the opportunity we provide. Instead of the cap, update the plan annually and incrementally while keeping the new goals in reach.

2. Don't change the comp plan so much that it doesn't look anything like it used to. If it turns out that your current comp plan is so backward that you can't modify it, and it needs a radical overhaul, then only make that change one time. Too much change too often will send people running for the doors.

3. Don't rush the change in comp plans. So, if it is November 15, and you want to start off the year with a fresh comp plan and bonus structure, etc., but you are only giving the team a few weeks to prepare for the change, that will scare them off as well. Make sure there is ample time to discuss, run what ifs, etc.; you want the team fully engaged and bought into the new structure.

4. Don't overload the base salary so that there really is no incentive to build and grow. Most people assume that any increase in pay is a worthwhile increase in pay. Wrong. If I live in an affordable area in Missouri, and my base pay is $85K per year, and my incentive comp is likely to add another $10K to 15K per year, I may say to myself, why work so hard? I live a nice life, my house payment is only $950 per month, and everything in my life feels comfortable. Why should I rock the boat to work so hard? The perceived amount of effort to gain the extra $10K per year might not be enough to push the envelope, especially as people get deeper into their careers and into the proverbial comfort zone.

5. Please don't overcomplicate the formula. If a sixth grader couldn't do the math, then your sales team might struggle with it, also. Adding too many qualifiers that could be perceived as out of their control may inspire suspicion and degrade the integrity of the relationship that you have with your team.

6. Don't base the comp on pure revenue. If the team is just paid on volume and total revenue dollars, that could cause them to bring in any kind of business and not the best kind of business. Please see the Client Retention Matrix for a greater explanation.

7. Don't worry about your compensation structure too much until

you have fully maximized the activity via the **30 Minute Success Plan** and you have the **10 Sales Systems** implemented. You can't correct sales dysfunction with a comp plan. All that ends up happening is you get people with big egos unwilling to participate in the structure, and you are too afraid or can't afford to undo the wrongs because you are dependent on that production.

Here's what I suggest—to the best of your ability, given the myriad of different types of businesses out there:

1. Do pay people based on **the gross profit dollars** they generate for the organization. That percentage varies widely based on your overhead. I have seen it as low as 1 percent and as high as 40 percent.
2. Do add accelerators for one to two specific goals. For example:
   A. If you exceed your annual GP$ goal by more than 10 percent, add a point to the comp, and
   B. If you exceed your annual goal by 20 percent, add three points to the comp.

   So a 15 percent commission becomes either sixteen percentage points or eighteen percentage points, depending on the level reached, and these incentives should go back to dollar one, not just on the amount of the increase. See the charts below for specific examples.

Example 1

Base Salary	Incentive Comp	Gross Profit Multiplier
$60,000/year	plus 2% of Gross Profit from $100K–$999K	plus 0.5% commission for any trailing 12-month period over 50% gross profit margin
$60,000/year	plus 3% of Gross Profit from $1.0M–$2.0M	plus 1.5% commission for any trailing 12-month period over 50% gross profit margin
$60,000/year	plus 4% of Gross Profit over $2.0M	plus 2.5% commission for any trailing 12-month period over 50% gross profit margin

Total Target Income: $180K

Example 2

Base Salary	Incentive Comp	Gross Profit Multiplier
$50,000/year	plus 3% of Gross Profit from $100K–$999K	plus 0.5% commission for any trailing 12-month period over 50% gross profit margin
$50,000/year	plus 4.5% of Gross Profit from $1.0M–$2.0M	plus 1.0% commission for any trailing 12-month period over 50% gross profit margin
$50,000/year	plus 6% of Gross Profit over $2.0M	plus 2.0% commission for any trailing 12-month period over 50% gross profit margin

Total Target Income: $210K

3. Do rotate in quarterly incentives that add additional rewards and keep the objectives fun. For example:
   A. **Q1:** all new clients that pay an invoice in the quarter add a $100 gift certificate to their favorite local golf resort.
   B. **Q2:** every referral that results in a first appointment counts toward a month's worth of weekly car washes for them and/ or maybe for the ops team and/or their family.
   C. **Q3:** every person who hits thirty new appointments in the quarter wins a weekend at the Ritz Carlton in Laguna

Niguel, California, and lunch with Chris Jennings (or not, in case that is not a motivator).

D. **Q4:** every lunch and learn or webinar run in the quarter that results in a new first appointment gets ten thousand miles added to their frequent flier program.

Keep thinking of fresh ways to incentivize the behaviors that you want, and don't worry if the reward seems too small, as long as it has real meaning.

4. Do personalize the rewards. If you are offering a trip to a resort, give people choices to pick Hawaii, California, or Vancouver. Some people don't love traveling to Vegas, but some do, so give them choices.

5. Celebrate the rewards publicly and at home. During the companywide gatherings, emphasize the accomplishment. Invite peoples' families to see them and/or send home a video with a prize for the family. For example, send a link to the awards ceremony along with a family meal for four sent to the household from their favorite restaurant so they can celebrate the rewards with the people who also likely made sacrifices, and get the family asking them for more of those meals.

6. Make this opportunity as good as or better than what they could find elsewhere. Put yourself in their shoes, and look for others' input in case your view of the world is jaded. *If I was that salesperson, do I have great reasons to stay? Are the financial rewards, flexibility, team environment, and administrative support all working well for me (them)?*

7. The basic formula is that the base salary is set at about "market rate" and that they should have the opportunity to double or triple their comp via commissions and bonuses. For example, if the base salary is $60K, they should be able to achieve an incentive comp of an additional $60K to $120K for total targeted earnings of $120K to $180K. In an interview, you can say

(depending on your state laws?) your on-target earnings should be between $120K and $180K; if your commissions aren't getting you over $100K in earnings, you won't be working here for very long. The higher the risk, the higher the reward. There are several places where there is no base salary or minimal base, let's say $30K, but the upside is big, meaning $250K to $1 million. In those cases, without base salaries, I would suggest one of two possible strategies:

A. Spot your new hires a draw for the first six to twelve months. That number may vary based on their requisite living expenses. If they need $8K per month to keep the lights on at home, I'm OK sponsoring that based on how well you know them to be able to perform, what the assessment results said about them, that they are committed to the agreed upon **30 Minute Success Plan**, and that is structured as a requirement to receive the draw, or

B. You have enough initial accounts to give the new person so that they can start earning a subsistence living in the first thirty days, so they don't have to worry about where their next meal comes from.

Please remember that compensation is just one aspect of the overall picture. How much fun they are having? What skills they are learning? How rewarded or recognized do they feel? Is the role in line with their future goals? Do you help them achieve unique meaningful connections with their coworkers and clients? What are the intangibles? If the list isn't long enough, it may not be enough to hold on to great talent.

Lastly, it isn't all about compensation; it may be that your sales team structure makes it very difficult for the individual team members to achieve their goals, so let's talk a bit about:

SALES TEAM STRUCTURE

One of my favorite things to do inside of an organization is to look at how all the interconnected parts affect the other parts of the company.

Ask yourself questions like:

- How many salespeople and business developers do I need?
- What sort of roles and responsibilities should the inside team, CSRs, and CXRs play?
- How many people should report up to one sales manager?
- Do I need a sales manager or VP of sales, or do I just need more salespeople?
- Are we efficiently using the human capital resources to maximum effect?
- Should I be buying leads for my team?
- Do I need to have an outside sales team, or could I run everything with an inside team?
- I need to build the department from the ground up? Where do I start?

I am going to answer all of these questions for you so you may complete your company **Sales Playbook**, or at least whatever version you are on today. It is really never complete, it continues to evolve, but by the time you are done with this read, you should have ample material to build your first draft, and beyond.

HOW MANY SALESPEOPLE AND BUSINESS DEVELOPERS DO I NEED?

So, you need as many productive people as you can find, sufficient to push your production team to 110 percent or greater than its production capacity on a regular basis.

In a perfect world, your operations team is never fully able to keep up with demand. You want to depend on the sales team to push you just beyond capacity on a consistent enough basis so you can freely invest in capacity, equipment, inventory, and all the other resources.

The sales team should **never** be asked to "slow it down." Nor should anyone ever say that or accept that as an excuse about why certain people are not following the process. You need at least 80 percent of the sales process implemented on a regular basis so you can predict sustainable growth and invest accordingly.

Each salesperson should pay for themselves by at least three times over what it costs you to pay them—if you are paying them $150K per year, they need to have the capacity to bring in at least $450K per year in gross profit, or this might not be sustainable.

Keep in mind, it will likely be one to two years to be fully profitable for both of you. The question is can you afford the ramp-up time, and can they? It won't be until year five that they fully start to realize their potential—so salespeople, don't quit before the miracle happens. Sales leaders, just make sure they are fully committed to the process and making progress by implementing all the systems already laid out prior in this text and make sure that you are fully implementing all the concepts from the Client Retention Matrix to get the full effect and have mutually rewarding payoffs to all concerned.

WHAT SORT OF ROLES AND RESPONSIBILITIES SHOULD THE INSIDE TEAM, CSRS, AND CXRS PLAY?

So, my favorite thing to do is to make sure that the outside sales team is counterbalanced by a complementary inside team. When I say counterbalanced by a complementary team, think balanced attack. A football team that only has good passing but no running game is sure to lose. A basketball team that averages 40 percent from the three-point line but can't score consistently in the paint is going to be easy to defend. Think balance.

Areas to balance include both teams being responsible for finding and winning new business while caring for existing customers.

I love setting up pods—smaller teams within a team. For example, in one "Pod" "Tiger Team" "Quartet" or "Fire Squad" (brand it to suit your company culture), I might put one to two outside sales-people, along with one inside salesperson, and assign that team an admin or back office support once the team exceeds $X million in gross profit. Both the inside and outside S/P are optimized for four hours per day **Go Live** time, and the back office person or people are getting the behind-the-scenes stuff worked out.

Every pod is required to and wants to cover for each other, every team is learning from each other, and there is some healthy competition between the teams.

Nobody on the team is superior to one another; they are equals in rank, and they all participate in the incentive comp, which would lean toward 80 percent individual comp and 20 percent team comp. This can also be a great way to develop talent and cross-train.

No matter whether you have a team component or not, I want the inside team to push the outside team, and vice versa—not all the pressure can come from above.

Pressure to perform needs to come from within. Let me repeat. Pressure to perform needs to come from within. Within the individual, and from within the team. Peer-to-peer accountability works way better than being accountable to a boss. Think internal drive and motivation that is a direct result of the process, systems, and structure that you create, and allow people to thrive inside of that process, system, and structure. They need to want this way more than you do for it all to work optimally.

HOW MANY PEOPLE SHOULD REPORT UP TO ONE SALES MANAGER?

DO I NEED A SALES MANAGER OR VP OF SALES, OR DO I JUST NEED MORE SALESPEOPLE?

Let's tackle these together and in reverse order.

Many companies try to hire a sales manager and/or VP of sales to help them build a sales department.

Odds are the people who would be good at building a sales department are not necessarily going to be good at running a sales department. Great sales leaders are always in short supply. If you are not willing to invest large sums of money to hire the very best talent, and you are hoping to get by for less, this likely will not work out.

Unless you have a huge infusion of capital, I suggest that you start with hiring sales talent. Quickly get to at least two salespeople. Being the lone salesperson in any company, especially if you are the first one, is going to be extremely hard.

Start with your **Special Teams players**. Perhaps, you keep going and just work through the **Special Teams** group, and you might not need to hire true outside salespeople. If you do hire outside salespeople, make sure you are getting four hours per day **Go Live**, or you are not getting your money's worth. If you are a salesperson reading this book, this comment is equally, if not more, important to you, so don't sweat what I just said; go get your four hours per day, and reap the rewards of performing at that level.

Now, most companies don't need to hire full-time sales managers until they get to four salespeople or more. If you have three or fewer, please follow the **10 Systems** to the best of your ability. If you get to the point where you have four to eight S/P or B/D folks on a team, then you need a full-time leader.

The sales leader is responsible for implementing the **10 Systems**, and if they are not implementing those systems, then you are not getting your money's worth out of that individual.

It may not be their fault. Perhaps nobody has ever taken them through the **10 Systems**; perhaps you are asking them to carry a territory in addition to the leadership responsibilities. If you are asking for them to do both, one of those two will suffer for sure, and perhaps both roles will suffer.

Are you loading way too many non-sales-related tasks or projects on their plate, and they now do everything half-baked?

Perhaps you violated the most known rule in sales leadership: you took your best salesperson and made them a sales manager. The odds of that working out are so slim.

Listen to me, please, on this point (by the way, I am speaking to all salespeople, sales leaders, and ownership or executive leadership):

great salespeople should probably stay great salespeople, earning large sums of money for the company, for themselves, and for their families.

People should only get into sales leadership roles if they are more motivated by helping others to be successful than they are by their own accomplishments. While this can change over time, for the most part, it is in our DNA. Look at your assessments and the motivational profile. If you haven't completed that yet, then please do so. Follow the link to our website ChrisJenningsGroup.com.

Don't dangle out "promotions" to good salespeople who are performing phenomenally when there is a good chance they will hate the leadership role and fail miserably. It can often turn into a demotion and cause people to leave.

Normally, players who were all-star players don't make great coaches. That level of performance was fed by a variety of incentives and drivers. Often the greatest coaches in sports were good role players, who were amazing students of the game, and are driven by team performance, not individual performance. Please ask yourself what drives you to perform. Look at your assessment results to see if the energy required will be put to good use. Please ask yourself what is most important to you.

There are exceptions to every rule, but getting this right will make or break the results.

Get outside help. From us, from whoever is solid. Stay a student of the game. Head coaches don't coach every position by themselves. They have specialty coaches for every role. Are you a head coach? Perhaps. Are you a high performer and occasional specialty coach? Perhaps.

I can't give you a one-size-fits-all from my desk as I write, but perhaps look at your **Goal Board**. Think about how you want to be spending your time. Get the systems built and then hire people to execute on those systems, and see if that doesn't yield the highest results with everybody being used to best purpose.

ARE WE EFFICIENTLY USING THE HUMAN CAPITAL RESOURCES TO MAXIMUM EFFECT?

Sales is a team sport. We work together in a coordinated approach for the betterment of the team so that the output of the whole team is greater than the sum of its parts. I think I am paraphrasing something that Herb Brooks said to the USA Men's Olympic Hockey Team hiring committee when he interviewed for the job prior to the 1980 Olympics, where the USA defeated the Soviets who had won the prior five Olympic Games in a row using the same strategy that coach Brooks installed.

There really are so few new ideas. It is about the implementation of solid basic principles applied to increasingly better effect over a period of time.

I believe I have covered quite a bit around using the **Special Teams players** to help the team. Balancing out the teams with the right people in the right roles doing the right activities with the right amount of frequency, while always looking at how we can improve our execution of said principle.

As I wrap up this section of the book geared toward sales leaders and true students of sales, I thought I should include the following.

10 Laws for Personal Growth

1. **Remain teachable.** Fight the urge to resist learning. It's what you learn after you know it all that counts.
2. **Get comfortable, feeling uncomfortable.** It's okay, it won't kill you. It means you are getting stronger. Progress, not perfection.
3. **Write and rewrite**. Your personal goals and visions you want to create. Reaffirm everything you deserve, even if you don't yet really believe that you do.
4. **Borrow from others that appear stronger.** Act as if you are them. Try on their confidence for size until it is really who you are.
5. **Find a source of strength outside of yourself.** Be it religion, nature, the gym, the piano; create a never-ending well to draw from.
6. **Use the old self-limiting stories** that lie within you as a reminder of what was, and be strong and faithful as you set your new course and rewrite your beliefs.
7. **Be grateful for every lesson that you receive.** Disappointment is always followed by a return to greatness. Take the lesson with grace and humility. Appreciate how far you have come and look with eagerness to who you are becoming.
8. **When your head tells you** not to show up, not to try, or not to commit or that you're already doing that, reframe and ask yourself, how can I do this even better? What simple adjustments could elevate my game to even higher highs?
9. **Stay humble.** There are many teachers all around; your coach, trainer, fellow student, boss, employee, prospect, child, parent, and random encounters are all brought to you to teach you something. Your job is to discover the lesson.
10. **Embrace sacrifice.** Invest in yourself. Give yourself the time - you are worth the investment. Even if it is hard to do, it all will bring you so much more. Open your mind to your future self. Let your dreams materialize; they always will, if you work for them.

chrisjenningsgroup.com

This is available as a download. You can print and post as you see fit. The more public, the more people will hold you accountable for the way we claim we want to live.

IN SUMMARY

With the right headcount, the right structure, the right CRM, a motivating comp plan, visibility to both activity and pipeline management, and a true interest in developing people, you are sure to become a leader all will respect, and your team will perform well beyond the norm.

It is a great honor to me that you are still digesting this material. I want to devote this final section to the people on the front lines of all sales arenas, offering a few other assorted tools to weave into the mix, grow with, and build upon.

PART 6

THE SALESPERSON'S TOOL KIT

———

This section is filled with some additional tools and nuanced strategies to keep your dialogue with customers authentic, effortless, and productive. It includes:

- Best questions to ask a customer
- Effective listening strategies
- How to quantify a problem or opportunity and have your prospect feel HEARD
- The power of the word "no"
- Offering choices and alternate options
- Being the adult in the room
- Staying humble, curious, and skeptical

BEST QUESTIONS TO ASK

I said it before, selling is at its best when designed as a conversation. I suggested that I could make these conversations go better. All conversations work better when we ask better questions and truly listen for and care about the answers to those questions, probably demonstrated by your writing down the answers to those questions.

I am going to give you some examples here, but I recommend you then highlight some that apply to you; they won't all apply. I am also leaving you space in the pages to insert your own. If you get out of this what I hope you will, you will read and reread, or review the pages multiple times over the course of the next two to twenty-five years as you continue to make your mark on this world and serve those you meet.

QUESTIONS ABOUT THEIR WORK:

1. How did you end up here?

2. Is this your dream job, or do you see yourself evolving into other roles?

3. How do you like the team around you?

4. What's your boss like?

5. How close are you to the people on your team (company, department, and office)?

6. If you had an anonymous suggestion box, what ideas would you give the company?

7. Are you able to get your work done inside of forty to forty-five hours per week?

8. What causes it to go beyond that?

9. Knowing I am new to the organization, what advice or direction would you give me?

10. How is the culture here?

11. Do you see yourself retiring from here?

12. What else should I know that I haven't asked that could make your life better here or anywhere?

QUESTIONS ABOUT THEIR FIELD OF WORK:

1. How did you get started in the field?

2. Where was your first job doing this kind of work?

3. How has the field changed since you started in it?

4. What attracted you to this kind of work in the first place?

5. How do you stay current in the field, process, or arena?

6. Do you participate in other groups or organizations outside of the firm that help you develop either new skills or relationships?

7. What's your least favorite part of this type of work?

8. What drives you to come to work each day?

QUESTIONS ABOUT MONEY, BUDGETS, AND COMPETITIVE PRICING:

1. How do you invest your dollars here?

2. If you were creating budgets for the company, what would your personal philosophy be?

3. How does that compare with what you are seeing?

4. How much time do you invest in collecting and reviewing quotes or bids?

5. What do you value the most in terms of response time, innovative thinking, creative thinking, industry expertise, and long-term versus short-term payoff?

6. What gets in the way of staying on budget?

7. What is the cost of delays versus the cost of getting it right the first time?

8. Everybody wants things done for less. How realistic are the expectations around what stuff really costs, and under what circumstances do you stop looking at costs versus payoff?

9. If we sent you quotes on three projects, and each one of our quotes was higher than the competitor's, would you even want us to still quote projects?

10. Let's pretend you do nothing different. What happens?

QUESTIONS GETTING TO THE HEART OF WHAT'S WRONG, OR WHAT'S POSSIBLE:

1. What brought us to this point?

2. How did you and I end up talking?

3. When did you first feel like this was worth looking at?

4. What got you to start to want to consider alternatives?

5. What else am I missing here?

6. Is there anything else that we haven't talked about that you think I should know? (Wait until you've been talking at least twenty minutes prior to ever using that question.)

7. On the off chance that we could improve upon what you are currently doing, where would you steer this conversation?

8. If I were just starting day one to work in this department, company, or initiative, what would you want me to know?

THE ART AND SCIENCE OF EFFECTIVE LISTENING

If you are going to ask questions, I encourage you to be very intentional about how you receive information.

Active listening is essentially the skill of repeating back whatever was shared with you to help your prospect or customer see that you are paying attention and validate what they offer you.

Sometimes you are repeating exactly what they have told you. Sometimes you are paraphrasing what they told you to make sure they know you got it, and if you haven't fully comprehended what they shared with you, this gives them a chance to further clarify their experience.

Additionally, as they share information that is either highly personal, important to them, and/or very important to how you might help them, I would suggest you add some.

CONVERSATIONAL CUSHIONS

These are essentially acknowledgments of what they have shared— you are recognizing what they have shared as an important piece of you better understanding them.

Think Prayer of St. Francis: "It is better to understand, than to be understood." Stephen Covey also highlighted this concept in his habit "Seek First to Understand."

Here are some favorite **Conversational Cushions** that should become part of your vocabulary if not already there:

1. I hear that so often.

2. Thanks so much for sharing that with me.
3. That sounds significant.
4. This helps me understand so much better.
5. I really appreciate you opening up to me.
6. I really appreciate you bringing that up.
7. That really clarifies your situation for me.
8. Your perspective is really critical to me.
9. Thank you.
10. Thanks for your insights.
11. That matters.
12. This is meaningful to me.

Please add your own; the list never ends and always evolves.

Following any of these **Conversational Cushions**, we really need lots of details.

A reminder **YOU ARE NOT BUGGING PEOPLE BY ASKING MORE QUESTIONS!** You are demonstrating that you care through your actions.

WARNING: this process will probably take longer than your current calls. Getting enough time to have a thoughtful conversation will be critical. If you are settling for ten-, fifteen-, or even thirty-minute meetings, one of two things, or both of these two things, will need to happen on the regular:

1. Book Your Meetings for Longer

Don't say this:

"I would love to get more of your time to share some of our exciting ideas with you."

If you are still saying this, please go back and reread this book, which by the way, I am guessing by your third time through, you should have a decent idea of what we are trying to communicate. If you haven't downloaded any of our podcasts, videos, or attended a program live in some form, try that as well. Make sure you are teaching this to others as you go, to strengthen your own convictions and personalization of what we are sharing. When I say "say this instead," you could say that verbatim, or you could use it as a template to get the flavor right and then make it your own. Let people get to know you and your style and see who clicks and who clashes. We can't all get along with everybody.

Say this instead:

"I'm going to suggest we book this for an hour just in case it turns out that we need that to get into some of the details of your situation. If it turns out we are done in thirty or forty-five, then you just picked up some breathing room to think between meetings."

2. Think of Your Sales Calls as the Next Episode in One of Your Favorite Shows.

Each time you get together with that person, prospect, or customer, do a recap from the previous "episode."

Highlight what you got out of it and emphasize some key points that were most important to them. Don't assume that they have been thinking about you nearly as much as you have probably been thinking about them.

Don't say this:

"I've been really eager to share some ideas with you and take you through our demo; you are going to love it!" Ugh, please don't say stuff like that. Be cool. Stay understated. Let the game come to you. Stay committed to your process and BeUseful.

Say this instead (after your hellos and your one to three minutes max of niceties):

"So, last time we were chatting, I picked up on a few highlights. (1) You were trying to accommodate the rapid growth, (2) it seemed like your team was feeling a bit overloaded, and (3) you were trying to onboard a bunch of more junior people at the same time. Did you get them all fully operational since we spoke?"

This last question is designed to get them to reflect on how much probably hasn't changed and remind them of why it's important that they are talking to you and getting some help. This also signifies that you were paying attention and have a good grasp on the priorities of what needs to happen to fix their situation.

Give them a few minutes to get into some of the details and let them fully appreciate how serious their situation really is.

One other important question to ask:

"Anything changed since the last time we spoke?" This way, if they are about to announce a merger, or they have a new boss, or their budgets were recently cut, it gives you a chance to pivot before you move the process forward based on outdated information.

Let's move forward with the detail questions. You have all seen the videos, or know this from your own family, of how little kids get into phases of asking a bunch of questions:

1. How come?
2. Why?
3. What's that?
4. Why not?

You could use some of those, depending on your tonality. Here are some of my favorite detail questions, which are sometimes better phrased as a directive:

1. I need to know more about _____.
2. I really want your perspective on _____.
3. Important because?
4. Interesting (followed by a pause, see if they fill in the space.)
5. Anything else there?
6. Could I get some more detail?
7. I'm very intrigued.
8. Always been this way?
9. Is this fixable?
10. Could you fill in some of the blanks for me?
11. How might that impact your situation?
12. What kinds of costs might you incur because of this?
13. Are you the only one here who feels this way?
14. How did this start, and when did it get more serious?
15. What happens if you do nothing?
16. Where does this lead you to want to go internally?
17. How might this make you (your team) look?
18. Any chance this goes under the radar?
19. Any potential impact on your career or image internally?
20. Are you still willing to work through this?

Pretty much any question is fair game **if it's relevant and not completely and overtly self-serving.** All these questions have to help your prospect, customer, or friend better understand the complexity and severity of their situation so that you can both—together—make an assessment of how to go about solving or mitigating problems and creating some sort of win/win/win outcome.

If the deal isn't win/win/win, meaning a positive outcome for you, your customer, and everybody else affected by your take on how to fix or improve where they are, then you need to tell them!

> Say this in those situations where you cannot see how to help them:
>
> "I'm not sure I can make this better."
>
> "I wish I could, but here are my concerns."

Then come back to my earlier advice.

If you see it, call it out, from how it will impact them, not how it will impact you. If they really want you to stick around, they may need to make an accommodation to get this to win/win/win. I'm not sure if that is a pricing, timing, logistical, or other type of solution, but there needs to be a high degree of surety that this will work, and if you can't do that, tell them the truth.

"Hey, there is about a 50-50 chance this works for you, and if you can't live with those odds, I should probably take my toys and go home, or am I missing something?"

DO YOUR PROSPECTS FEEL HEARD?

Before suggesting any solutions to any problems, we suggest that you quantify the extent to which your prospects are experiencing their issues, problems, and opportunities. Once again, we are employing a simple acronym—**HEARD**—which stands for:

- Hours
- Emotions
- Adversity
- Relationships
- Dollars

You always want to be able to step back from the situation and say to yourself, *If I was this person, I would certainly want to get help from us or somebody like us.* There really needs to be an overwhelming amount of documented evidence that a change is warranted.

The sum impact of HEARD must outweigh the discomfort and cost of the change

Again, the agony of making the change (employing your solution), needs to be far less than the agony of remaining in the same boat. This must be quantified. Here we go.

HEARD: Hours

I want to know how many hours a week, day, month, and year they are investing to fix the issue or deal with the issues. I want them to calculate for me their time invested as well as the amount of time that anybody else in their organization is investing. Once you get a total number of hours dealing with whatever the challenge is, you can ask some great follow-up questions around the severity.

Don't take for granted that if they say they are burning five hours per week dealing with the problem, they are feeling it yet.

Don't say this:

"It must be horrible putting all that time into it; I bet you have better things to do with that time."

Say this instead:

"Sorry to hear that. Is that what you thought it would be? If it weren't for what you experienced, how would you use that time?" or "How should that time be spent across the organization?"

For example, if you sell recruiting or placement services, and you identify that your prospect is spending five hours a week reviewing resumes and interviewing candidates that don't meet the requirement, let them give you those details; don't bail them out too early with some overstated promise assuring them how time efficient they will become after they start using your services.

Let them appreciate their own situation. Let them feel it a bit before we go into a solution. That is where the "E" comes in.

HEARD: Emotions

With every event, there is an emotion attached to it. Don't be afraid to weigh in on the emotions, and I might suggest that without your prospect owning and sharing some of their emotions around their plight, your connection to them will lessen.

If they feel comfortable describing in detail their level of frustration, their fear of not resolving it, and their disappointment and embarrassment for allowing it to continue on their watch, then you know they are starting to trust you. You are making them feel safe to share openly and certainly increasing the odds of them feeling safe in hiring you as well.

This really should serve as a measure of their attachment to the issue and their willingness to work through it. Nobody does anything until the suffering gets bad enough. Additionally, fixing it has its own level of suffering, so we have to know where they are.

HEARD: Adversity

I am sincerely interested to know the level of adversity they have encountered along the way. It goes to the complexity of their issue.

If I go back to the recruiting scenario and we identify that your prospect, the hiring manager, has been wasting about five hours per week reviewing resumes from other recruiting firms that are constantly sending unqualified applicants. They are getting behind on other work, such as performance evals, and now are faced with working over weekends when they should be spending time with their families and investing in their own personal health, but they have been sacrificing sleep to keep up with the workload. Now that they are sleep-deprived, they haven't been as communicative as they'd like to be with all the people in their life at home or at work. This sounds like real adversity and a problem that, over time, has taken a toll and needs a different solution. This is what I mean by adversity.

They expected one outcome and have been met with another. Anytime one's expectations are out of alignment with their reality, they are experiencing adversity. Some of that adversity is now likely showing up in their relationships.

HEARD: Relationships

So often, the adversity encountered starts to affect not just the person we are talking to but all the people around them. Often in larger organizations, one's reputation is so critical to them, and if their relationships suffer, that could be career limiting; it could be affecting their customers, their colleagues, their boss, their peers, their direct reports, and other people in other departments. It is always critical to understand the many relationships that might be impacted.

The issue you are solving for could impact both professional and personal relationships. Maybe they are coming home later and leaving their partner to shuttle kids around on their own; maybe they are sacrificing time with close friends, not going to a yoga class or poker night. Maybe it's a hobby that is suffering, meaning they don't get to that basketball league they enjoy so much, and somebody else has replaced them in the starting lineup.

In the movie *The Devil Wears Prada,* there is a great line where Anne Hathaway's character is complaining about how she might miss her boyfriend's birthday party to attend a work event. Her colleague in the film, played by Stanley Tucci, has an amazing revealing comment in response. He says, "Don't complain to me; once your entire personal life has gone up in flames, then you will be ready for a promotion." It is often a sad but true statement made by many trying to accomplish a lot at their work.

If you truly understand the details of their adversity, you are gaining trust, and you are positioning yourself in a great spot to really help them. If you don't know the level of detail, you may just be throwing stuff at the wall.

The last, and sometimes most compelling, quantifier is dollars.

HEARD: Dollars

How many dollars is the lack of performance, issue, shortcoming, or unrealized opportunity costing that individual and their company? Yes, I said costing that individual buyer, as well as what it costs the company.

Don't say this:

"I bet this is costing you a lot of money to run so inefficiently." No, no, no.

Say this instead:

"The situation you are in is starting to sound really unpleasant, and I appreciate the detail you are sharing. Out of curiosity, have you calculated the rough costs in dollars as to what it's running you to not _____ (fill in the blank with problem du jour)? "

"Also, curious to know, this doesn't affect you personally in any way financially? Lost bonus, reduced incentive comp, etc.?"

Check your tonality but get the details. Download our video podcast on approaching these conversations at our website ChrisJenningsGroup.com.

Once you have truly **HEARD** out your prospect or customer in detail, and you are convinced beyond any shadow of a doubt that they need to do something, and you handled the conversation in a tactful but direct way, you are getting closer to your prospect becoming a customer, and you becoming a real trusted advisor. I am including this chart for you to document the details with each prospect or customer.

What Is the Impact of These Issues?

Customer:

	Detail	
H ours		
E motions		
A dversity		
R elationships		
D ollars		

HOW COMMITTED IS YOUR NEW PROSPECT TO ADDRESSING THEIR ISSUES?

This section is optional and may or may not apply and/or feel comfortable to you, especially if your tonality isn't spot on.

I might suggest that, most often, our biggest competitor is "complacency." Fear of change, trying something new, trusting another human being when our history shows us that others have failed us—all of this gets jumbled up into vague levels of commitment from our prospects.

Prospects often offer mildly encouraging comments that lead us to believe this is happening when the prospect isn't yet truly committed. They say things like:

- I like what you have shown me.
- This could work for us.
- Let me run this up the flagpole.
- Let me work on getting this in our budget.

These are all nonbinding compliments that often go nowhere.

So, at some point, you have to have "The Talk." Yes, The Talk about commitment, to see if their interest level in doing this is anywhere close to what your interest level might be.

Now, if and when you decide to have this talk, there are a few key questions I suggest you bring up with your prospect somewhere **just before, during, or potentially after** your demo or presentation and **Letting them Know You and Your Company.**

Don't say this:

"If I could show you a way to improve your situation, would you commit to a purchase order," or, "I want to earn your business, and I would like to get an order before I leave today."

Say this instead:

"After learning what I have about your situation, I am starting to see some real potential for us to make a contribution toward solving what you have experienced to date."

"Considering how fortunate I am to have been through this (dozens, hundreds, or thousands) of times, I have a pretty good idea of how we might help. The biggest issue tends to be around how committed we both are to working through this. Your situation, as you have explained it to me, isn't an easy thing to fix. I already know my commitment level to addressing these issues, and I do this work because of the impact we have on people's lives like yours. I guess my real question is, how committed are you to working through this? Like I said, it isn't easy."

They will likely say, "I am very committed." If they don't, you have bigger problems—go back to BeUseful...Now and start over, because something was missed along the way.

Here is how I measure commitment:

1. **Are you willing to change** and try something completely different than what you have done in the past? "You have been with your current supplier, vendor, or partner for several years. How willing are you to go in a different direction?" Make them prove to you they could leave their current provider without issue or hesitation. If they can't, start over and go back to **Setting an Agenda** in **BeUseful...Now**.

2. **Are you willing to commit the time** involved in working through the change? "Our average implementation goes on for one to three months and will probably require one to two hours per week from you and perhaps your staff or team to get

through the implementation inside of XXX weeks, and I need to know, are you open to that?"

3. Lastly, are you willing to find the funds? "Can you make what appears to be a larger investment than what you initially thought this would be, including getting sign-off from your CFO, CEO, and others who initially handcuffed you with a smaller budget?" Again, we need a clear pathway to the finish line.

4. Lastly, (I am intentionally saying lastly again, in case your situation requires this fourth added component): "I know your IT team was pushing back on this initiative as a lower priority originally. They won't have to do all the heavy lifting; we do that, but I do need a couple of project managers to schedule one to two hours each week for the first sixty days until we are fully operational. If we can't get that commitment, I don't think we should move forward."

Essentially, I am trying to point out to you a way to get to what needs to happen in any deal.

The customer has to want this more than you want this. If at any point in the deal, you want this way more than they do, then the deal is out of balance, you are going to look like a pushy salesperson, and it's going to get really awkward.

When I said let the game come to you, this is what I meant. There are so many prospects out there that likely desperately need what you offer that you shouldn't worry about what happens in any one deal.

Regardless of the size of the deal, if this is a $3 million deal, treat it like it was a $3K deal. Treat it with relaxed confidence.

Let the game come to you!

THE POWER OF NO, AND HOW TO INFLUENCE WITH INTEGRITY

I believe that the longer we are alive, the more important it becomes to figure out what to say no to. Earlier in our lives, we appear to have a lengthy time horizon and thus get a vast sampling of situations to help us shape our morals and decisions, and create better lives for ourselves and those around us. Over time, we must learn to say no to more people about more things, including, in some cases, our customers.

This can be a foreign or difficult concept for so many of us positive, optimistic, and open-minded sales folks, and striking a balance here is important.

Also, this concept is important for us to help our customers sort through what is a priority initiative and what really isn't. I don't think we should ever feel hurt, sad, or disappointed if we helped somebody decide to do an about-face and go in a different, and perhaps more advantageous, direction.

I want us to bravely look at what is best for our customers—to come at it from the perspective of them making a change by hiring us as more of a long shot or low probability but worth exploring to help them figure it out.

I don't need to tell you that they have done a decent amount of research prior to talking to you, and just because they are now interviewing three providers, their best choice might be to do nothing at all. Let's at least stay open to that as a possibility.

Once again, please don't be an obnoxious, sarcastic "push away" salesperson, where the prospect can see from a mile away what you are trying to do.

Don't say this:

"Now, if what I have to offer isn't going to suit your needs, I can just leave," or "I would hate to see you miss out on this," or "Our prices are going up next week; you are going to feel pretty bad if you miss out." Please, nothing cheesy, manipulative, or sarcastic!

Say something like this instead:

1. "I'm not sure how applicable this might be to you, but I thought it was a worthwhile exploration."
2. "Given the number of options you have, I thought it would be worth looking at where we fit, and perhaps we don't."
3. "If it turns out that making no changes is best for you, let's keep that open as an option. If it ends up looking like a change is required, let's see if I can help you figure out where we fit, if anywhere."

Remember, these strategies are best applied with a delicate touch and not to be over-used. Think about salt as a seasoning: a little bit makes lots of foods taste better. If you go overboard with salt or any other communications strategy, then odds are you ruin the meal.

Some of you are asking yourself, at this point, *Doesn't this weaken my position? Isn't it going to scare away the prospect or customer if I don't sound positive about what I do and how it fits?*

My general answer to this is as follows: I want you to have a high level of conviction in what you do, how you do it, and why you do it. The area of doubt is really centered around the prospect being a good fit, at this time, for what you do. So your puzzled and curious approach should center around how well you fit what they need at this moment in time, given their circumstances.

I want to remind you to be highly confident in yourself and what you bring to the table. I want you to remain open to all the possibilities and let the game come to you. **Trust in your process, stay curious, stay humble, and stay confident.**

A FEW MORE STRATEGIES REGARDING THE POWER OF NO

All good conversations have a natural flow to them. Conversations made easy stay open, vulnerable, and willing to lean in where required. This isn't just in sales, mind you.

In some cases, you will run into "The Contrarian." For those of you who remember or want to Google the Life Cereal commercial with Mikey: "Give it to Mikey, Mikey doesn't like anything." Remember, or can you guess what happens?

Mikey ends up liking the cereal.

Again, this strategy will work best if used in the honest and open subtleties of getting to know someone without presuming any outcomes.

I really want you detached from the outcomes. Let the game come to you.

So, the other ideas and strategies:

All good conversations should stay in balance. In some cases—e.g., The Contrarian—it is usually one person's job to say yes, and another person's job to say no.

Too often, as a salesperson, we come in "pushing" and "selling" our ideas prematurely, shooting low percentage shots that get swatted away by disinterested or prematurely negative reactions to our ideas from our prospects. Better to switch roles and allow them space to say yes.

A safer way might be to start with an unassuming proposition.

For example, say this:

1. Not sure this comes up for you (followed by their issue)...
2. This may or may not apply in your case...
3. Not sure if this resonates with you...
4. Wouldn't know how often you run into _____ if at all?
5. This could be a stretch, but...

6. At the risk of sounding presumptuous...

7. Perhaps unlikely in your case...

And so on. Think of this again like a cushioning agent to the tougher question. Allowing your customers to come toward you and not be scared off, overpowered, or offended by you degrading or belittling their work to date.

Describing perfection is another way to go. So, if you were offering managed IT services:

> **Don't say this:**
>
> "Bet you have the smartest-ever IT people working in your company, and nothing ever breaks or goes wrong." That just sounds so obviously manipulative and gross.
>
> **Say this instead:**
>
> With a very neutral, open, and non-sarcastic tone, "A company like yours has likely had a solid IT provider for a while, and if your network has never had any security breaches—known, or unknown—and all your software and hardware upgrades are seamless and without incident, and your IT resource returns all your calls within five minutes every time with somebody who not only knows what they are doing but actually can carry on a good conversation, then there is probably very little I will be able to do to improve your circumstances."

This is a very honest statement. It suggests that changing when it's not broken isn't useful. If there is little or no upside payoff from getting an outsider to at least look under the hood, then we should get out of their way and let them go back to work.

Again, being completely unattached to the outcome but very interested in helping them are keys to **Conversations Made Easy**. So please check your tonality and your body language as you deliver this kind of language. It's a fine line between sounding like an open, honest, vulnerable industry expert and a disinterested, unmotivated jerk.

Odds are, you can't tell the difference on your own. So please **record your phone calls** and Zoom calls, video your trade shows, and capture live examples of how this is playing out for you. If you can get us live examples, we can iron out any wrinkles pretty quickly. If you are doing this without any feedback from a third party, it's going to be hard to pick up all the nuances. Stay vulnerable. Stay teachable. There is no telling what great things can happen as a result of making all your conversations go easier.

BUBBLE WRAP YOUR IDEAS

One additional way to lean on "no" and still make brand new suggestions to your prospects is to safely offer your new idea **"Bubble Wrapped."** It's a way out for the prospect if they don't have a level of interest.

If you have something new, different, perhaps bigger, bolder, or completely off from what the customer is asking for, but you know, as an expert in the industry, that it will help them, then **Bubble Wrap the Idea**—think allowing them to opt-in, and make opting out as easy as opting in.

> **Don't say this:**
>
> "You're going to hate this, but I really want you to install this new version of Jabber, unless you don't like Jabber." Nope. Wrong. Awkward.
>
> **Say this instead:**
>
> "I'm not sure whether you're going to like this suggestion, but I couldn't live with myself if I didn't bring it up. If you were willing to install the latest version of Jabber and let my chief engineer look at the code you have been writing, we might be able to save you two to three steps. If you are completely closed to the idea, I certainly don't want to force this on you; we can definitely keep other options open."
>
> Think of this like giving them a soft and safe place to land in a difficult stormy situation.

Or,

> **Say this instead:**
>
> "I know last time we chatted, upgrading to the latest version of Jabber was completely off the table, and if that is still the case, I am going to turn left real quick with something else, but before we let this go entirely, I wanted to at least do a check-in with you."

Stay curious, open, or even a bit puzzled.

Allow the game to come to you. Don't be afraid to lean into areas, even if they were flat-out rejected in the past, if you have really good reasons to bring them up. Then **Bubble Wrap the Idea** and lean in. At the first sign of hesitation, give them an out. If they are serious about doing anything with you, they will likely come back toward you in a more open and honest way, which allows you to make a closer connection and get to the truth.

GIVE PEOPLE CHOICES

Most often, it is easier to give your customers choices about areas we could lean into. There are often multiple areas, and a wise person would start at the high-priority items for their customer and work from there.

Don't say this:

"Whatever you want from us, we can do it. If you can think of it, we can execute." Again, real people don't really talk that way; only cheesy salespeople do.

I've said it before, if you are talking to your customers and prospects any differently than you talk to your friends, families, coworkers, and all the other people in the world that you interact with, whatever you say could come out wrong.

Say this instead:

"Ravi, I'm glad we're chatting. This could end up being a really short conversation, but on the off chance there was something going on that we could help with, I wanted to reach out. Now typically, when I'm working with a company like yours, they are reaching out to us for one of the following situations:

1. They keep getting annoying test intrusions, looking for a way in that don't look like cyber spies, or
2. They have had minor outages in the network, or
3. Since they sent their teams home, the network keeps getting stressed with a mix of legit work, and/or personal searches, or
4. They are just trying to stay two steps ahead of the cyber criminals out there.
5. Any of those resonate or is your situation completely different?"

This really allows people to opt-in to an interesting, relevant conversation that feels easier on both parties.

As you become more advanced in your conversations, the goal is to make them easier to have for both you and your prospect or customer.

Constantly put yourself in their shoes. What must it be like for them in their role, with their experiences, with their goals, and see if you can fit yourself to be of maximum service to them. Keeping a servant mindset, without devaluing ourselves and what we bring to the table, but an openness to **BeUseful...Now**, with a belief that all my **Conversations Can be Made Easy**, and that each conversation with another human being is uniquely shaping my skills, knowledge, experience, credibility, and confidence.

WHEN YOU GET TO THE END, AND THE ANSWER REALLY IS NO

I don't expect to win every game; in 2020, the Tampa Bay Buccaneers lost five of their first eight games on the way to winning the Super Bowl against an excellent Kansas City team that had beaten them handily earlier in the season. In fact, I would suggest it was because of that loss that they were able to win the Super Bowl, and perhaps this may apply to you as well.

So, when it's a no, you have three things to learn from this event. **Three more questions to ask:**

1. What could you do better, differently, more, or less of?
2. Who could they connect you to?
3. Under what change of circumstances should we talk again?

> **Don't say this:**
>
> "So, my boss is going to be on my case 'cause I couldn't close this, anybody else you could give, and I'm going to keep your number and call you again in thirty days, just in case you change your mind."

As I write this stuff out, I'm thinking how ridiculous this sounds, but I promise you, these exact words are being spoken somewhere right now. It's no wonder people want to buy from the internet when the human experience is so distasteful. But with just the right amount of salt, it can taste a lot better.

Say this instead:

"Jan, I really did enjoy getting to learn so much about you and your company, and I can't help but feel there were certain areas that perhaps I could have shed a better light on what and how we do what we do. Any chance you would be kind enough to honestly share any pointers or suggestions you would have for me?"

After learning as much as you can here, picking up clues she may not have shared earlier in the process:

"Thanks for that, Jan. I'm curious, having gotten to know us a lot better, not sure where you think we might be better suited? I don't know if there are other divisions here, friends of yours from prior places you worked, other industry events you frequent, where you might point me?"

Listen again, keep learning. This career is played out over a very long season; Jan might hire you at her next job. She might be starting that next job next month and not yet able to share that with you.

Lastly:

"Jan, I am hoping this works out really well for you, and if, for some unforeseen reason, it turns out you need help down the road, these would likely be the reasons." (Give her the most likely negative outcomes and disappointments.)

- The lower cost labor they bring in ends up causing more delays, or
- The tolerances are not to spec, even after your team has signed off, or
- You open that other facility, and you want to run us as a comparison to what you are going with now.
- Is there anything else I haven't thought of that you would want me to know?

Stay open, and get the lessons. Every single time things don't go the way you wanted, there is a lesson to be learned, and so often, the lesson is far more valuable than the account.

You will work hundreds, perhaps thousands of opportunities over your career. Stay a student of the game, elevating your skill level—the growth potential for all of us is unlimited.

BE THE ADULT IN THE ROOM

Growing up has its pluses and its minuses. It is summer right now, and I often feel that even as adults, we long for the summer vacation we had as kids—maybe consciously or maybe subconsciously. It's difficult to know when our subconscious is taking over our actions, thoughts, and feelings.

UNLESS WE HAVE AWARENESS OF WHAT TO LOOK FOR

I am going to take a few moments to share a school of psychology called transactional analysis, first developed by Eric Berne, who published a book called *Games People Play*, that helps name specific influences that shape how we communicate in any human interaction with a spouse, coworker, client, etc.

Berne noted that in our developmental years from birth to seven years old, the people who raised us had a significant impact on the people we would become as adults, significantly influencing how we interact with other people throughout our lives.

There are **three primary developmental stages**:

1. **The Parental stage**, which is divided into two influential patterns:
   A. **The Critical Parent**, who barked orders at you.
      ◦ "Don't chew with your mouth open."
      ◦ "Get your elbows off the table."
   B. **The Nurturing Parent** who was affirming, caring, and offered reassurances like:
      ◦ "Your artwork looks nice."
      ◦ "It's going to be OK."
      ◦ "You were really brave."
2. **The Adult stage** where we learned reason, very simple conclusions that we could make based on facts.
   A. "If I touch a hot stove, it hurts my finger a lot."
   B. "When I eat too much candy, my stomach hurts."
3. **The Child stage**, which was divided into three influential patterns:
   A. **The Natural Child**, which was a very innocent and pure form of:
      ◦ "Let's go play."
      ◦ "Can we build a fort?"
   B. **The Compliant Child**, who was fearful of conflict and tried to create harmony to avoid scary and stressful situations that overwhelmed them as a small, mostly defenseless child.
   C. **The Mischievous Child**, who liked to play practical jokes on their siblings or others. They liked to stir the pot.

I am guessing as I describe these, you may already have been able to identify who in your upbringing left you with this psychological imprint, and you can probably see the tendencies play out in all your interactions with others.

I know I can, for sure. My dad was much more of the Critical Parent, and my mom was the Nurturing Parent with a loud Natural Child, and I have a good mix of them all.

By the way, your prospects also had the same psychological imprint that heavily influences how they treat you. In a sales environment, as well as any healthy communication, it should all be what I call **"right down the middle lane."**

ADULT TO ADULT MIXED WITH A HEALTHY AMOUNT OF NURTURING PARENT

Any communication that comes from the Critical Parent, or any of the Child states is likely to work against us and not for us or for our audience.

Often, we as salespeople inadvertently slip into one of the Child states.

Don't say this:

"Wouldn't you love to try out our new product?"

"We have a super good sale going on right now, and you can save lots of money."

"This solution is going to be the greatest thing you have ever tried."

Can't you just hear the child in us? I know your prospect or customer can, and it does a lot to degrade the quality of our relationships. This kind of interaction only leads to a loss of self-respect and the respect of our customers.

> **Don't say this either:**
>
> "Sure, I can call you back later."
>
> "Let me check with my boss and see if I can get you a discount."
>
> "I wish I could lower the price, but my company won't let me."
>
> "I would be happy to requote that for you in different quantities and then drive the samples over to your house on Saturday."
>
> "I hope you got my voicemails from last week and that you had a great weekend, so sorry I missed you."

Can't you hear the scared little child that comes across? It's not pretty. It's not helping you. You are no longer that small, defenseless child, and it's time to be the adult in the room, even with your prospects. In fact, especially with your prospects and your customers. They are hiring you to be the adult in the room.

> **Say this instead:**
>
> "I would imagine the last thing you want to do is go through a new software implementation, but given everything you just told me, I am wondering how you can avoid it?"
>
> "I wish I could tell you there was a way to invest less and make this work, but my guess is if you try to shortcut this now, it's going to come back to haunt you in a multitude of ways. Let me explain how."
>
> "Sure, I can get you a quote. Tell me first how you and your team would use this if we did move forward, and out of curiosity, why didn't your team join us today? Are you the only one in the department who has this on your radar? Does that seem right to you?"

Another way to paraphrase this type of interaction is to follow this formula:

- Read the room for what you see, hear, and can feel is the truth.
- Recap for your prospect what you think you are hearing, even if it is a tough message.
- State it from how it impacts your customer or prospect, not how it impacts you.
- Say it nicely.

Be the adult in the room. Keep it down the middle lane. Adult to adult, and Nurturing Parent to adult. Take your kids out to play on weekends, find ways to forgive your critical parents, and let that go.

Last tool in the tool kit for now:

STAY HUMBLE, CURIOUS, AND SKEPTICAL

Maintaining an insatiable urge for more knowledge can only help you. Taking a sincere interest in every prospect in a very genuine way will pay countless dividends.

Staying completely detached from the outcome of any sales call and only wanting to better understand will invite lots of great information coming at you. You don't have to be the expert. You don't have to be the smartest person in the room. Acting like you are when it really doesn't matter will only work against you.

Humility doesn't mean that you lack confidence. Humility means that you stay open to all possibilities, that you have the openness of a young child with an insatiable curiosity about how things work or don't work in your customers' lives.

You can be very confident and very humble; that is, again, my favorite combination.

Don't be a know-it-all; do want to learn more.

Don't assume that your assertions are all 100 percent accurate and applicable; do stay open to what you can learn from every conversation.

Take a sincere interest, take notes, pause, slow down, and thoughtfully probe for more details. Reference the details you learned from the last call, and ask follow-up questions.

If you didn't think of everything in one meeting, call them back.

> **And say this:**
> "I was reviewing my notes, and I was super intrigued about your point referencing _____." (Something they said you noted.) Then ask them another question.

As often as possible, **keep the conversation live, not on email.** Tonality goes out the window when we email, no matter how often you read it back to yourself.

It's OK to be ignorant about specific details in their circumstances. You can know a lot about the industry and not much about them.

Don't say this:

"I have learned a lot over my ten years, and I can tell you for certain _____."

Say this instead:

"I'm ten years into this and still learning something every day. I was curious, how long have you been _____?"

Relax, take it easy. If they have nervous energy and you mimic that, things get tense.

Set the tone with a relaxed confidence that you can handle this. You are super intrigued by the details of their story, their work environment, their career, and their purpose, and then look for the natural intersection of your purpose and their purpose.

Take your conversations to a higher level by not settling for surface conversations.

Ask for permission to dig a little deeper and remind them that their story matters immensely to you and see if you don't become a really important person to them. A true partner. Place their wants and desires ahead of your own and see how many people will be drawn to you and the relaxed way you engage them.

THIS IS THE ESSENCE OF
CONVERSATIONS MADE EASY

Humble—not a pushover

Confident—not arrogant

Understated—not overbearing

Relaxed—not anxious

Open—not single-minded

Friendly—not schmaltzy

Informed—not a know-it-all

Focused—not rushed

If we put these on a continuum, we should always be moving closer to the ideal and looking for feedback from those that know us well about areas for improvement, and maybe we should be completing our assessments to accelerate your progress in the right direction.

CLOSING COMMENTS, ALIGNMENT, AND WHAT TO DO NEXT

I hope at this point that most, if not all, of your questions received answers and that as you journey forward, you keep this as a reference tool for the many situations you encounter.

- **Part 1:** Where we gave you a conversational model in **BeUseful... Now** to use as a guide to make your conversations easier to have.
- **Part 2:** Where you built out a specific plan detailing the variety of **activities** in the specific quantities necessary to achieve all of your goals.
- **Part 3:** Where you took **ownership of the stories** you tell yourself and started to write newer, brighter stories that will serve you today and going forward.

- **Part 4:** Where we outlined the **10 Sales Systems** to build championship-caliber teams and a way to objectively monitor your progress.
- **Part 5:** The **Sales Leaders Tool Kit** gave you nuanced examples of the most common roadblocks that occur in assembling a great team and how to work through them.
- **Part 6:** The **Salesperson's Tool Kit** filled in the blanks on just about every remaining scenario.

I have mentioned that sales really is a team sport. Every quarterback gives credit to the offensive line. Every defense improves when the offense increases its time of possession. No salesperson will ever truly achieve their real potential without the support of a great team around them.

So, if you are the offensive coordinator, you need to talk with the executive team and figure out what's the best way to have the highest performing team.

I usually like to pair outside people with an inside team. I don't really want the inside team to feel subservient to the outside team; it should feel like a partnership. Perhaps one inside person could be teamed with two to three outside people. That depends on your group.

Both groups should probably have a team element to their compensation and an individual element. They should be able to call each other out when things go wrong. They should be working out of the same playbook.

If the playbook isn't clear to the team, the leader owes it to them to clarify the plays and work on better execution and the best utilization of assets.

Administrative help can be crucial. There is a bit of chicken or egg to consider. Any sales professional should be able to produce with or without admin help, but don't overload them with too many administrative tasks that they might be bad at.

If your company won't hire that kind of help, consider if you, as a big producer, and perhaps other colleagues on your team, should all pitch in and hire a resource on your own.

The main point is **four hours a day of Go Live** time has to be possible to achieve the top results, and it won't make any sense to limit yourself. If you are spending seven hours a day doing admin and only an hour a day talking to prospects and customers, then your system is broken, and you need help.

Sales development representatives, lead developers, and junior team members—there are lots of situations where younger or newer people to the business get to cut their teeth working the phones, email campaigns, and other strategies.

Perhaps they shadow a very experienced, highly productive individual, and over time, they take over certain accounts—that works as well.

Sales engineers, technical experts, executive team members, and other **Special Teams** players all matter a lot. It may not be all of them. Sometimes a great engineer who has no desire to talk to customers should stay a great engineer. However, pick the people in these groups that you want in front of your customers. Set up some real specific strategies about when they come along, what their role is, and how they fit into the success of the team.

Bringing along the owner, CEO, or chief engineer can do a lot to solidify what might otherwise be overlooked opportunities. Create a cadence for everyone, and hold everyone accountable. It shouldn't be up to just the leader. The peers, direct reports, and new people should all be able to point out upside potential—don't ignore their advice; embrace it.

WHAT IS RIGHT IS SO MUCH MORE IMPORTANT THAN WHO IS RIGHT.

THE HARD THING TO DO AND THE RIGHT THING TO DO ARE TYPICALLY THE SAME.

Make this a team that people want to play on, and more great players will look to get traded to your team. Invest your time, money, and other resources into helping your team grow to achieve heights they could never have achieved prior to joining your team, and see what loyalty is really about.

CLOSING COMMENTS

I am sitting at LAX again, waiting for a delayed flight to take off for Vancouver. If all goes well, tomorrow, I will get to spend the day with an incredible group of both super new to sales, mid-career folks, and some seasoned pros.

They have great potential and are well on their way to doing something great in their marketplace.

This company has a history of investing in its team and developing their skillsets. People tend to start off in more junior roles and then quickly get more and more responsibility. They call on some of the largest companies in the world.

They are hungry to learn, grow, and improve, even when they feel overwhelmed.

So many of their people that started as account executives are now running larger teams of their own. They work hard to pass on the lessons they learned, and even in a brutally competitive market, they regularly outperform their competitors.

I don't think it's an accident; I think it's by design. They have set an intention to hire bright, motivated, positive people who often start out a bit scared and intimidated by their customers. They quickly steel up their spines and establish a mutual set of boundaries that leads to better outcomes for their customers.

The company is cool, fun to work at, and profitable. People are held accountable. All the results of every person who works there are on display for all to see.

They often shrink territories to help increase the results that each account executive gets out of each account.

They are good people who work hard but keep a balanced life. The egos are held in check. The leaders are humble, confident, supportive, and honest.

The compensation is lucrative. The company is profitable. The clients are super happy with the results.

They regularly dedicate about one to four hours per week to working on getting better.

It's how a company should be run. There are many reasons why this ideal doesn't materialize, but I feel like we are all selling ourselves short if we don't work toward it.

I don't want to retire in the traditional sense. I love being engaged with the clients we support. I am rooting for them to realize their dreams and goals. I am rooting for you to realize your dreams and goals.

It's all out there for you. I hope I have made this seem within reach for you, because it is.

I hope I get to meet you and you share with me what this book did for you. If I don't get to meet you, and you just read this book and put it all into action on your own, fantastic. If you end up diving into our self-driven programs available online, or you get to work with one of our partners on our team for some personalized coaching, that's also fantastic. We have such amazing people, who not only have good answers to your sales challenges, they have big hearts and a sense of purpose.

We are here for you. When and if you are ready. There really is no limit to what you can accomplish. I am honored that you have included us on your journey, and I look forward to walking the pathway alongside you and the many others you may share this with.

Humbly yours.

Chris Jennings

Made in the USA
Las Vegas, NV
01 June 2023